BATCHWORTH PRESS

ASSYRIAN PALACE RELIEFS
AND THEIR INFLUENCE ON THE SCULPTURES
OF BABYLONIA AND PERSIA

A PERSIAN RELIEF FROM THE LOUVRE

TEXT BY R. D. BARNETT — KEEPER OF
THE DEPARTMENT OF WESTERN ASIATIC
ANTIQUITIES IN THE BRITISH MUSEUM
— ILLUSTRATIONS SELECTED AND
PHOTOGRAPHED BY WERNER FORMAN

BATCHWORTH PRESS LIMITED

ASSYRIAN PALACE RELIEFS

AND THEIR INFLUENCE ON THE SCULPTURES OF BABYLONIA AND PERSIA

GRAPHIC DESIGN : BEDŘICH FORMAN

DESIGNED AND PRODUCED BY ARTIA FOR
BATCHWORTH PRESS LIMITED
SPRING HOUSE · SPRING PLACE
LONDON NW 5 · BP 101 — S 132
Printed in Czechoslovakia

THE ASSYRIAN PALACES AND THEIR SCULPTURES
IN THE BRITISH MUSEUM *by R. D. BARNETT*

The Assyrian Palaces form a series of monumental buildings covering the 9th to the 7th centuries B.C., of great importance in the history of ancient art and civilisation. In Mesopotamia from earliest times the Royal Palaces (in which dwelt the city's King, who was the god's bailiff or representative, his vicar on earth) seem to have been regarded as of almost equal importance with the temples of the gods and the *ziggurats* or temple-towers. These buildings often form a single architectural complex. If one wishes to understand something of them, one must glance briefly at the long history which they have behind them. By the time the First Dynasty of Babylon was established under the Great Hammurabi in the 18th century B.C., the Royal Palace has developed from a private house built round a courtyard into its classical form of palace, consisting of a series of rectangular courts surrounded by elongated rooms. It is significant that the Assyrian word for palace, *ekallu*, is derived from the Sumerian word E. GAL, "the great house".

From earliest times the entrances or interiors of Sumerian temples are adorned with figures of animals, such as lions, or bulls, carried out in fresco painting or metal work in high relief, and evidently intended to drive away evil, while the inner walls of the temple might bear scenes of human figures painted in fresco technique.[1]

This system of decoration was further developed. At Mari, on the middle Euphrates, large figures of seated lions, cast hollow in bronze, protected the doorways of the Temple of Ishtar, and appear frighteningly lifelike.[2] The less wealthy, provincial Temples had to reproduce such figures in clay.[3] Meanwhile, in the King's Palace at Mari, complex scenes in fresco were painted on the walls. One represents a king in Heaven, surrounded with sphinxes and mystic trees. Fragments of other scenes of procession and sacrifice survive. Such ideas of decoration, deeply involved with magical notions of keeping away evil, were transmitted at an early date to the Anatolian plateau in the North. For, by the 14th century B.C., the Hittite Palace at Alaja Huyuk has colossal figures of sphinxes in its gateway. We also meet here for the first time reliefs beside the gateway carved in stone. Their subjects are of three kinds: hunting scenes, scenes of ritual and, perhaps, the capture or escalade of a city.

Meanwhile, in Assyria the palaces of kings were still decorated only in fresco. The earliest palace known is that found by a German expedition in 1913-14 at the site of Kar-Tukulti-Ninurta, founded by Tukulti-Ninurta I (about 1250 B.C.), near Ashur. In this palace were panels painted in polychrome fresco, illustrating scenes of goats and sacred trees—a routine motif then already ancient, probably connected with the cult of Ishtar.[4] The panelled style is perhaps connected with similar painted panels found at Nuzi; but by the time of Tukulti-Ninurta we can see that the tide of influence which formerly flowed into Anatolia from Mesopotamia, begins to flow back from Anatolia; for Tukulti-Ninurta's predecessor Shalmaneser I (c. 1280 B.C.), is the first King of Assyria to imitate from the Hittites the art of writing historical annals or yearly records, in fact consisting of the king's military achievements. It may well be, too, that he (or one of his dynasty) was the first to introduce from Hittite lands into some Assyrian palace, now lost, the Hittite custom of flanking the palace gateways with mighty figures of sphinxes or other composite beings carved in stone. For, at least from the 9th century onwards, this was the custom in Assyrian palaces, where the walls are also embellished in a further manner which must surely be of Hittite origin: with reliefs of carved stone, depicting ritual scenes or illustrations from the king's battles and triumphs.

The tradition of decorating gateways with carved stone slabs along the walls, the openings being equipped with figures of large lions, was well established in North Syria by the beginning of the Iron Age, and must therefore go some way further back in time. But not only lions are used in this position. Thus, at Carchemish on the Euphrates, a part was found of at least one human-headed bearded gateway-lion,[5] while the Syrian provincial palace at Tell Halaf, perhaps of the 10th century B.C., has female sphinxes, griffins and a scorpion-man carved in the round in its doorways.[6] Assyrian palaces, however, prefer as their gateway-figures human-headed, bearded and winged lions or bulls. In the wall decoration, there is also a close connection between Assyrian and North Syrian traditions. The North Syrian-Hittite sites have usually orthostat (dado) slabs, showing a rather elementary composition of two or three figures, often arranged symmetrically—a tradition derived from the art of Sumer. At Malatya, however, we have an important innovation—the series of small carved slabs, showing ritual and mythical scenes, was raised high up in the wall, becoming a decorative frieze,[7] thereby moving closer to the Assyrians' use of the sculptured narrative frieze. What we have, in fact, in the architectural decoration of these two areas, amounts to close affinity rather than identity, and very possibly goes back to a common ancestry in provincial Babylonian and Mitannian buildings of the Middle and Late Bronze Age, of which we know nothing at present, and can only speculate. Much might be learnt from the excavation of modern Tell Arban, a large Assyrian site low down on the Habur river, if it ever were to take place. This was certainly originally a Mitannian fortress, probably to be identified with a city called Shadikanni. Ashurnasirpal of Assyria seems to have occupied Tell Arban in the 9th century B.C. and built here a palace, which Layard, seeking the site of Nineveh, located in 1850, but he got no farther than finding some gateway figures[8]—a human-headed bull and a lion of curious style. But whatever the contacts between Hittite, North Syrian and Assyrian architecture may originally have been, by the 8th century B.C. there is no doubt about them, for Assyrian kings from Tiglath-pileser III onward explicitly claim to have modelled parts of their palaces on the plan of a Hittite *hilâni*, and it seems they mean by this a building, or part of one, which you enter through a portico between free-standing columns supporting a loggia or upper floor with windows.

It is worth noting that the custom of decorating palaces with fresco paintings did not die out with the advent of sculptured decoration. At Til Barsip in North Syria, in the palace of the provincial governor were found a series of splendid polychrome frescoes showing scenes of lion hunting and triumph over prisoners, as well as ritual figures and decorative ornaments. These frescoes which practically completely perished after discovery (except for some fragments now at Aleppo and Paris), belong to the time of Sargon (late 8th century B.C.).[9]

In the larger Assyrian palaces, however, fresco decoration retreats into a subsidiary place, to decorate doorways, or to ornament unimportant rooms with patterns and conventional motifs.

From the rise of the Assyrian kingdom at the end of the Bronze Age, the building of palaces seems to have been not merely a tradition, but a regular royal occupation, perhaps even a ritual duty. It seems to have been the ambition of any Assyrian king of importance to build himself a fresh palace of his own, even if (as did Esarhaddon at Nimrud)[10] he might perhaps use some of the sculptures of a predecessor.

It has been pointed out[11] that at Nineveh there were palaces belonging to as many as thirteen kings, between Shalmaneser I (circa 1280 B.C.) and Ashurbanipal (late 7th century B.C.).[12] Of some of these palaces, often only traces survived, in some cases amounting to nothing more than an inscribed brick—claiming to be from the palace of King X, King of Assyria, but still proving its one-time existence. Now Nineveh was only one of the great capitals of Assyria. The number of palaces was probably no less at Ashur and Arbela, for there would have been nothing strange in a king having a palace in each. Several of these kings, whose palaces stood

at Nineveh, certainly built others also at the site of Nimrud, where much excavation has laid them bare.

* * *

Nimrud is the Assyrian city of Kalhu, or Calah, as it is known in the Bible.[13] The name of Nimrud is the Arabic form of that of Nimrod who, according to the tradition recorded by the Hebrews in the Book of Genesis, was the mighty hunter, father of Ashur, eponymous hero of the Assyrian race. Nimrod was said to have founded Nineveh, Calah, and two other cities, the sites of which we do not know. Nimrud is perhaps merely a corruption of the name of the Assyrian deity Ninurta, sometimes spelt Nimurta, patron god of Kalhu, revered as a god of hunting and of war. Calah, or Kalhu, was certainly a very ancient town, though it is unlikely that its origin goes back as far as Nineveh. But it was occupied by Shalmaneser I, whose palace, Ashurnasirpal informs us, had fallen into decay, and had to be completely demolished. The palace of Ashurnasirpal, often called the North-West Palace, discovered by Layard in 1848,[14] is the earliest Assyrian palace which is both tolerably well preserved and published and, rightly or wrongly, as far as we can see at present, seems to be the first of the classical type of grandiose Assyrian palaces, decorated with monumental gateway figures and relief carvings. Layard found its plan to consist basically of a complex of narrow rooms grouped round a square court—following the ancient Mesopotamian house-plan. But it has been shown[15] that the full plan of an Assyrian palace really consists of two such courts, called the *bîtânu* (derived from *bîtu,* a house or inner court, reserved for the private life of the king, his harem and personal servants, and the *babânu* (derived from *bâbu*, a gate) or outer court, to which the king's subjects and others had access, and where official business was transacted. The palace, as found by Layard and as published in plan, consisted of but one court, the *babânu*. But it is clear that there was also a second, outer court on the North side, linking the *babânu* and the complex of temples around the foot of the *ziggurat* consecrated to the god Ninurta in the corner of the mound. This outer court, however, has been eroded away into a ravine by the rains of centuries washing down from the mound. But the recent excavations of Professor M. E. L. Mallowan have recovered the court's Northern edge and the fine North entrance to the palace, ornamented with reliefs showing Phoenicians bringing gifts or tribute in the form of monkeys, strange creatures from overseas which seem to have been much prized in ancient Mesopotamia. As these merchants approach, they appear to be saluting, or perhaps executing a dance, snapping their fingers, a gesture with which the Assyrians sometimes greeted their gods[16] (pls. 9, 13).

On the North side of the *bîtânu* was the Great Hall (Room B), conveniently entered from both courts. The throne was placed before a great sculpture in relief at the narrow end of the room, showing the king twice, standing on either side of a "Sacred Tree" between winged spirits who anoint him magically. On another wall were great slabs bearing magnificent figures of the king, surrounded by his court officials, his Cup-bearer, the Keeper of his Bow, and his eunuchs (pls. 28, 29). On either side of him again stand the beneficent winged spirits to protect him, anointing him with some magical substance which they dispense with a fir-cone out of a bag-like vessel

(pl. 28). These figures have a majesty and immense deliberation which places them in the forefront of ancient art. All that is accidental has been purged from them, leaving them only with the essential. It is to be noted that, though designed on so large a scale, yet the dresses bear, faintly incised, many tiny decorative scenes representing embroideries, which can hardly be seen without close study. It is possible that they were originally picked out with coloured paints—for colour was certainly originally used in these and other Assyrian reliefs, a point which shows the close relationship between reliefs and fresco painting in Assyrian art. On these slabs, traces of black and red still in fact survive on the shoes of the figures, having apparently been protected from weathering in antiquity by accumulation of rubbish or soil on the floor of the ruined hall. White filling of the eyeballs also remains in some instances.

Along the South wall, for the whole length of the room at about eye level ran a sculptured series of a different kind. This was a double band of scenes showing the king, no longer in calm repose, but in vigorous action, either engaged in scenes of warfare, in which he is ever victorious (pls. 10–25), or hunting wild bulls (pl. 27), or lions (pl. 26), both of which once abounded in the Mesopotamian marshes. The wild bull (Assyrian *rîmu*) was known as far West as Palestine (Hebrew *reëm*), the Psalmist alluding to the skipping of its young (*Psalms*, XXIX), while the lion abounded, the last lion in Mesopotamia being killed only in 1896.[17]

With Ashurnasirpal's scenes of war (though such scenes were well known earlier in Assyria),[18] we meet for the first time in Assyrian architecture the attempt at portraying *narrative*, of recording a *sequence* of events, which have to be conveyed in terms of space by a continuous frieze unrolling like a scroll.[19] An earlier monument, the so-called White Obelisk of Ashurnasirpal[20] had pointed the way, by depicting events in repeated scenes on different sides of the obelisk, to be followed in a spiral movement, like Trajan's column. But here they are all on the same level, and the effect is closest to that of a "still" film, the king, the hero throughout, being seen in a number of successive actions, leading his troops against the enemy in battle or in siege or on the march (pls. 10–25). Which city or what nationality he is to be imagined attacking in each case, is far from clear. The cities are not labelled with an identifying inscription, and the details of the enemy's dress are to us vague and unspecific, though they were probably obvious enough to the Assyrians; one scene has been recognised as depicting some Iranians, perhaps a tribe of Scyths from Ashurnasirpal's eastern campaigns;[21] other scenes suggest his campaigns in the West, which carried his arms to the river Euphrates. This impression is strengthened by the tribute of elephant tusks which the defeated or surrendering city proffers, since elephants then still haunted the Euphrates and its tributaries, till they were hunted to extinction chiefly by the Assyrian kings themselves in the 8th century B. C. The broad river which the troops are fording with boats or with the aid of inflated goat-skins could well be the Habur, a tributary of the Euphrates (pl. 16).

The upper and lower bands of reliefs were originally separated by a broad band, inscribed with a cuneiform text. This is the so-called "standard inscription" of Ashurnasirpal,[22] so termed because it is found repeated countless times, probably for magical reasons, on the walls of the North West Palace, carved neatly but with complete indifference to the subject, right across the reliefs of court or ritual or on the bodies of the great gateway-figures. In it Ashurnasirpal vaunts his greatness, his military exploits, his invincibility, his building of the palace, his piety and devotion to the gods. When these narrative reliefs were found by Layard, orders were given to saw off this text from each of the slabs, so as to lighten the load to be transported home to London. A surviving line of the text, however, can still be seen above or below many of the slabs as now exhibited, and illustrated here.

The upper and lower row of scenes are mutually connected in the case of the hunting scenes (thus we have, above, the lion hunt; and below, the libation and sacrifice after the hunt over the dead carcase of the lion). But an exact correspondence between upper and lower series in the military and triumph scenes is hard to establish. It seems that to the Assyrian viewer the exact sequence of events did not yet greatly matter.

Halfway down the wall of the throne room was an exit, flanked by massive figures of winged genii, executed virtually in the round. Such figures in these palaces have, besides a technical function in supporting the door lintel (perhaps arched) on their wings, a religious or magical purpose, to keep away from the king's residence evil spirits and noxious influences, the warding-off of which was an obsession to the Babylonians and Assyrians. These gateway figures were called *lamassu* or *šedu*[23] and are usually of monstrous size, winged, with the head of a bearded man, wearing, however, a headdress with horns to indicate his divinity. Their bodies are either those of lions or bulls, and for good measure they are provided with five legs, two to be seen from the front, three from the side. Of course, this excessive number is not meant to correspond to a fact, but is merely due to the awkwardness of fusing two planes, indeed the extra leg is only noticeable from one angle: but it cannot be ruled out that it is meant to imply two stages of action, the monster moving, then coming to a stop. Round his loins he carries a girdle with a slip knot. This is a leash as used on hounds or hunting animals, and indeed it is still used on hunting-cheetahs,[24] or used to be. It indicates that that creature is ready to be unleashed to pounce on an evil spirit at a moment's notice.

It is probable that the reliefs, no less than the gateway figures, all had a magical purpose. Certainly the remaining relief slabs from the throne room, showing a winged male figure holding a goat and an ear of corn or a stag and a branch (pls. 1, 2) have some such significance.[25] As to the remaining rooms of the inner court, Rooms H and G were banqueting halls. Behind them lay two small suites, I-J and M-L, the walls of which were sculptured with reliefs representing winged deities, eagle or human-headed, performing a magical ritual of anointment of a "sacred tree" (pl. 7). It would appear possible that this is a sort of maypole decorated with symbolic leaves, representing the god Ashur, patron god of Assyria. Ashur is seemingly assimilated to Tammuz, the beloved of Ishtar (perhaps alluded to in pl. 3), spirit of vegetation, who dies annually but is restored to life by sprinkling with the water of life. The analogy of the rooms in the palaces at Til Barsip[26] and Arslan Tash[27] strongly suggests that these rooms I-J, M-L, were sleeping rooms, watched over by these protecting spirits, while a perforated stone slab in the floor of each room served as a drain for a washing place or lavatory. The same arrangement of rooms occurs on the south of the court.

* * *

In the world of the Babylonians and Assyrians, anything that could occur, particularly to the monarch, might be fraught with ominous significance, and could be construed as a harbinger of the gods' intentions, good or bad. It is not surprising if the monarch's slumbers were particularly important, and we can see from the Biblical story of Joseph, how in the kindred world of Palestine and as far afield as Egypt, dreams were deemed to be an index of God's will and the monarch's dreams, in particular, a veiled forecast of the future. Not far from Nineveh Ashurnasirpal II dedicated[28] a temple to Mamu, the god of dreams, and built a palace called Imgur-Bêl—so named after one of the defensive walls girdling the city of Babylon. The site, now called Balâwât, was discovered and excavated by Hormuzd Rassam, the former assistant of Layard, in 1878, and doubts which were unjustly thrown on the veracity of his account[29] have lately been completely dispelled by the excavations in which Professor Mallowan in 1956 reopened the site. The remarkable feature of this temple and palace was that their double doors, probably of cedar wood, were ornamented with horizontal bands of bronze, embossed and chased in relief with narrative scenes like miniature versions of the stone sculptures ornamenting a palace. Rassam discovered at Balâwât one pair of such gates set up by Ashurnasirpal II, which were, unfortunately, very much damaged, and also another pair, almost perfect, set up by his son, Shalmaneser III.

In 1956 Professor Mallowan was fortunate enought to find yet another pair, also of Ashurnasirpal, still in position in the temple, and to work out the plan of the little building.[30] Rassam's gates of Ashurnasirpal have never been published, except for two bands.[31] The remaining sixteen bands were recently found uncleaned and in fragments in the reserves of the British Museum, where they had lain forgotten until 1956. They are now being prepared for publication at long last. They form the decoration of two gates originally about 3′3″ wide and at least 11′ high. The scenes include both representations of hunting and battle scenes (e.g. the capture of Bit-Adini), and scenes of tribute-bringers (e.g. from Carchemish). The gates of Shalmaneser, however, which are both larger (each 7′6″ wide), and excellently preserved (pls. 137–173) contain scenes only of his campaigns and triumphs. They number eight a side, six of each being in London, the rest divided between Istanbul, the Louvre, Boston and the de Clerq collection. As hinges were unknown to the ancient world, doors were attached to a door-pin which was held by a ring at the top to the wall and pivoted at the bottom in a depression cut in a stone. In the case of the Balâwât Gates, these door leaves were evidently hung on a massive door-pin of rounded shape, which must clearly have been a trimmed tree trunk with a diameter of 14″, and the bands are curved to fit round it. As they are of slightly varying lengths, it is obvious that they should be arranged to fit the taper of the tree trunk with the longest at the top, and the shortest at the bottom.[32] The correct arrangement or something like it appears to be as follows (not as illustrated in the present plates):

Year	Expedition	Year	Expedition
?	West	849	Syria
858	Sea	850	S. Babylonia
858	Unki	854	Supria
858	Carchemish	860	Urartu

Year	Expedition	Year	Expedition
850	N. Syria	860	Van
857	Urartu	859	Tyre
854	Hamath	851	S. Babylonia
853	Kulisi	858	Dabigu

From this list it will be seen that the designer—or at least the bronze-worker who carried out the work—paid little regard to chronological order of the events depicted. It is probable that the bands were not mounted one close above the other, but spaced at intervals of some 3–4 inches, making the total height of the door about 13 feet. These gates may be rightly hailed as among the surviving masterpieces of ancient metalworking, though for the skilled Assyrian artisans they were probably merely a routine exercise. They offer us in great detail a fascinating wealth of information, not only about the Assyrians, but about the appearance and equipment of the Assyrians' great enemies the Urartians or people of Urartu, the Biblical Ararat, who lived round Lake Van in Eastern Turkey, about that of the Tyrians, Hittites of Carchemish and other foreign races, who are all, fortunately for us, identified by a line of text in cuneiform giving the campaign in which they were encountered. Most interesting, too, are the scenes showing Shalmaneser's march to the source of the river Tigris[33] where he sacrificed to the gods of the river and set up a carving (pls. 143–45). Less pleasant is that we meet for the first time illustrations of the barbarous punishments meted out by the Assyrians to the enemy, afterwards a commonplace in the military scenes of the successors of Shalmaneser (pl. 159 d). It is this lack of restraint and the exclusively one-sided obsession with the king's glory that marks the sharpest difference between Oriental art and classical Greek art. Bronze decorated gates were not unknown elsewhere in ancient Mesopotamia—Sennacherib set up a pair at the *akîtu* temple of the Plain for the shrine called E-balagga, and describes in great detail the mythological scenes of the battle between Ashur and Tiamat which they bore.[34] Fragmentary remains of further "bronze gates" were also found at Khorsabad, in the royal palace of Sargon.[35] But why was there so great a profusion of bronze gates at Balâwât in the temple of the god of dreams? Were they a record of the royal dreams which had come true? We are irresistibly reminded of the passage in Homer, which tells us that dreams have two gates. The one pair are of horn—through them pass the dreams which come true—while those dreams which are but illusions pass through gates of ivory.[36] A curious point of fact is that Professor Mallowan found evidence that his gates had stayed open for very long, indeed, had jammed in that position. Was this an accident? It seems unlikely. It is not the only example from the ancient world where the opening or closing of Temple gates had a symbolic significance. The gates of the Temple of Janus at Rome were closed only in time of peace. In fact, it is recorded that the Emperor Augustus was the first person to close them, since it was the first time that peace had reigned on all Rome's frontiers for two hundred years. The militaristic Assyrian state did not include in its calculations a state of peace, unless it were the peace of exhaustion; there were few years which were not marked by a campaign in one quarter or another. Well might the doors of their Temple of Janus (if such it was) become fixed in their position.

War, in fact, was the principal activity of the Assyrians, partly, it must be admitted, enforced on them by the natural weakness of their geographical situation. Hence it is not surprising that warlike subjects figure so largely in these sculptures and bronzes. Indeed, we learn from them and the extraordinary detail of their illustrations, more about the Assyrian military machine almost than from any other source. The army seems to have been under Ashurnasirpal and Shalmaneser III merely a militia, raised from the Assyrian citizens. But Shalmaneser in his wars in Syria made heavy demands, and it is recorded that at the battle of Qarqar against the coalition of twelve Syrian kings[37] in 854 B. C., he led 120,000 men. This must have been a *levée en masse*, a conscription of the entire available manpower, clearly exceptional. The different arms of the army seem to be distinct, well equipped and organised. There are light infantry bowmen, mounted bowmen, and chariotry, carrying bowmen armed with a spare lance, also mounted lancers (pls. 161, 167). An interesting development of Shalmaneser's is the provision of units of picked bowmen protected by heavy coats of mail (in fact, leaf-armour) which reach down to their feet, giving them an appearance very much resembling Norman knights. The effect, in fact, of these bronze strips as a whole is strangely similar to that of the scenes on the Bayeux tapestry depicting the conquest of England by William the Conqueror.[38] Indeed, the notion is not so far-fetched, for the Bayeux Tapestry may be considered the lineal descendant of this school of narrative art evolved by the ancients.

These heavily protected archers are used by Shalmaneser as a sort of bombarding artillery, under cover of which the lightly armed storm troops and pioneers can assault the city (plates *passim*). It is clear that the art of siege warfare, using mines, battering rams and siege machines and the construction of siege-mounds was highly developed by the Assyrians (pls. 140a, 159a, 162a) and they could ford rivers either with skins or by building pontoons (pl. 162c). The usual use of the siege machine was to approach under cover of arrows sufficiently close for the loose-slung ram it contained to break down the enemy's battlements. Only twice on the bronze gates we see a ram of different type with a boar's snout (pls. 140a, 162a). The usual armament of the soldier was a pointed helmet, light shield and spear or bow, but one branch was trained in the use of a screening shield (*arîtu*), at first small (pl. 168), later enormous, which was placed to protect the light archer when firing. The army built protected camps of two sorts, round and square (pls. 141a, 161c, 156a, b, d) like those of the Roman legions, the round type being seemingly more favoured by the chariotry. Slingers were apparently used only by the enemy in Shalmaneser's time, but by the time of Sargon (late 8th century B.C.) the Assyrian army had a large force of them, as he was able to settle in Kummuh (S. E. Anatolia) no less than 1500 cavalry men, 20,000 bowmen and 1000 slingers as military colonists. Tiglath-pileser III, the creator of the Assyrian empire, greatly expanded and reorganised the army, by the wholesale introduction of colonial brigades led by the provincial governors, who greatly resembled the later Persian satraps. As a result, many new types of men and equipment appear in the sculptures. The resulting army seems to have been threefold, the king's regular army or bodyguard, partly trained levies (*kisru*) and the colonials. Large numbers of prisoners too were regularly drafted into the Assyrian army. The units seem to have been built up on tens under an N. C. O., or *rab esertê*, fifties under a *rab kisrî*, and hundreds perhaps under a *rab sarîs* or *rab mugi* (cf. *Jeremiah* 39, 3). The commander was the *rab-shakê* (who makes an ugly appearance before Jerusalem in the time of Hezekiah, II *Kings*, 18), the commander-in-chief was the *turtanu* (Hebrew *Tartan*) (*Kings*, ibid.), who no doubt operated in the king's name in the innumerable battles where the king invariably claims the victory as his own. The similarity throughout to what is known of the Persian army and its organisation is noticeable, and it is clear that the Persians inherit it from the Assyrians, in the main. Through the Persians, the Assyrians' ideas on military matters were transmitted to the West, becoming the common stock of much of Hellenistic military training.

Shalmaneser III built no palace at Nimrud, as far as is known. His main residence was surely elsewhere. Apart from some colossal bulls at Nimrud, we have no architectural sculpture from his reign, the only comparable work being the famous "Black Obelisk" bearing the scenes of tribute, including that of Jehu, "son of Omri", the king of Israel. On this monument, scenes of tribute and of wild life are illustrated (pls. 32—34). But the monument, in spite of its great Biblical and historical interest, cannot be said artistically to break any fresh ground. After Shalmaneser, the Assyrian empire passed through a century of defeats, internal disturbances and decline. A few stelae and some statues in the round are all we have to illustrate the continuity of the dormant sculptor's art until we come to the period of Assyria's resurgence under the new military leader, Tiglath-pileser III (745—727 B.C.), who restored the Assyrian empire and carried his arms across the Euphrates through Syria as far as Palestine. By the Hebrews he was sometimes known as Pul (2 *Kings*, XV, 19). Tiglath-pileser gives account of the sumptuous palace he built at Nimrud, giving it a portico (*bît-hilanî*) patterned after a Hittite Palace.[39]

When Layard excavated the site of Nimrud, he found nothing left of Tiglath-pileser's palace, except the sculptured slabs which had once adorned it:[40] they were found stacked in heaps, ready for re-use in an unfinished palace which Esarhaddon had planned to build some sixty years later. The conditions of discovery would make it difficult to visualise the original arrangement of these slabs but for two series of detailed drawings made at the time of discovery, some of which have been recently published.[41] They appear to have been set up (in imitation of the long frieze of Ashurnasirpal) in a double frieze, the upper band being separated from the lower by a band of text with a cuneiform inscription. There are battle and siege scenes (pls. 35–8), tribute scenes, scenes of the king enthroned and of foreigners surrendering—Arabs (pl. 39), Gileadites,[42] Urartians[43] and others. As in the North West Palace, there are also slabs with a single row of large scale figures in addition to those of smaller scale in the friezes. But what strikes us is that neither set has the majesty or the surety of touch, nor indeed the boldness of design, of the older school of Ashurnasirpal, though they are not without dignity and vigour. But they have a kind of rustic, rougher look. One feature differing from Ashurnasirpal is that the king is no longer shown much as an ordinary man, a *primus inter pares*: instead, he and his courtiers and companions-at-arms are depicted like giants or demigods, half as tall again as the ordinary soldiers (pl. 40). With this new elevation of the king above the ordinary level goes the increasing interest in depicting scenes of impalement, mutilation and brutal torture of the captives.

The ascent to the throne of Tiglath-pileser's son, Sargon (or Sharrûkîn) (721–705 B. C.), was a milestone of importance to the Assyrian state and its art. By taking the name of an almost legendary predecessor of the distant Babylonian past, Sargon II proclaimed his imperial ambitions from the start. After a series of brilliant campaigns in which he totally defeated his Urartian neighbours, who had formed a dangerous threat to the North and North East, and established a firm control over the region to the North West, he set himself to build a new palace at a site previously untenanted by royalty, the site of a village called Magganuba, 15 miles north west from Nineveh. The palace which he called Dûr-Sharrûkîn ("Sargon's Fortress") was built with the utmost care and splendour, and on a scale never till then attempted. Sargon succeeded in creating a building of monumental scale, in the decoration of which the greatness and dignity of an absolute Oriental despot was for the first time truly mirrored. Dûr-Sharrûkîn, in modern times covered by the mound called Khorsabad, was the first of the Assyrian palaces to be discovered, falling to the credit of a Frenchman, Paul-Émile Botta, in 1843. He and Victor Place, who succeeded him in 1850, were able to excavate it and publish their results with the aid of ample funds provided by the French Government. The sumptuous publication of Botta in five volumes[44]—now an expensive rarity—with its beautifully engraved illustrations, gives the fullest picture we possess today of a great Assyrian palace. The whole city formed a vast square enclosed within walls about a mile long, its points orientated to the points of the compass. In the North West Wall was the hill on which lay Sargon's palace with a *ziggurat*, and in the South West corner a group of temples, which Place mistook for the Royal Harem. The façade was decorated in coloured tiles with a curious group of figures—a lion, a raven, a bull, a vine, a plough; this apparently was the name of

Sargon or of his palace, written in some strange form of rebus: "Coloured clay pictures in the form of the stars, the likeness of the writing of my names" is the description which Esarhaddon, Sargon's son,[45] gives of these strange pictograms, undoubtedly conveying some astrological equivalents to the syllables of his name, which remain still a riddle. In the palace gateway were *lamassâtê*, protective winged, human-headed bulls of unexampled size, four at a time, grouped in pairs at right angles to each other, vigilantly scanning the approaches to the palace. Other similar figures, with a winged deity behind them anointing them magically with a pine-cone, stood within the gates of the citadel; a pair from the South East Gate in this wall have been, since 1849, in the British Museum, another pair from the South West Gate is at Chicago, a result of the American excavations of 1934, which re-explored the site. On the façade of his palace, Sargon, again apparently imitating the contemporary neo-Hittite custom of North Syria, incorporated carved orthostats. Within, he greatly extended the decorative system of his predecessors, carving the walls of the South West wing with scenes usually in two rows, separated by a band of cuneiform, in fact, his Annals up to his fifteenth year. The sculptures show his military conquests, scenes of tribute, and banquets. Gone are the "standard inscriptions" of Ashurnasirpal, gone too is the defacement of sculptures by the text being written straight across them, like a surcharged postage stamp. Practically gone, too, are the ubiquitous winged eagle-headed figures of the earlier period. In style, there is now a sureness of touch and a sense of composition hitherto missing. Differences of dress of different racial types are noticed more and more. Each block of stone is no longer a self-contained unit, but the

narration continues straight across them, though a room might still contain on its walls more than one subject; thus, the attack on the city Harhar, the burning of Bît Bagaya, the attack on Tikrakka all appear in Room II.[46] Other rooms show more-than-life-size figures of king and courtiers, captives and tribute scenes. The king and his eunuchs, executed in an unusually high relief, have an almost portly dignity. In the building of this palace Sargon took the deepest interest, and several cuneiform letters from his archives survive, in which he gives orders for, or receives word of, the progress of the work, the bringing of great stone thresholds from Parsumash, or the setting up of the *lamassu* figures.[47]

* * *

After Sargon, Dûr-Sharrûkîn ceased to be a royal residence. But Sargon's son, Sennacherib, sought not merely to emulate his father but to surpass him. He decided to make his capital at the city of Nineveh, already an ancient site with a history of at least three thousand years when the prophet Jonah, the son of Amittai, in the middle of the 8th century B. C., walked in its streets and prophesied punishment to its inhabitants and to its king.

Here Sennacherib, on the South West corner of the citadel now called Kuyunjik, built a splendid residence, which he boldly named "The Palace Without a Rival", and which it fell to Layard and his successors to explore a hundred years ago. Sennacherib's palace was an enormous building containing over 70 halls, chambers and passages, as far as it was excavated by Layard and his successors, of which almost all contained sculptured walls. It is hardly surprising that the money at Layard's disposal did not suffice to publish all the vast number of sculptures which he discovered, and consequently, in his great work, the *Monuments of Nineveh*, (1st and 2nd series, 1849 and 1853), we have only a selection of the carvings from the palace of Sennacherib. A later scholar, Archibald Paterson, published in 1915 a single volume, *Assyrian Sculptures: The Palace of Sinacherib* (now a rare book), in which he tried to bring together and publish or republish in proper order all the sculptures from this palace. But even this work is quite incomplete, as many of the sculptures, now lost or reburied by their excavators, are known only from unpublished drawings to which he did not have access. It is hoped to remedy this situation as soon as possible.

The sculptures of Sennacherib's period show in one way advance, in another way decline from the high level of Sargon. The figures are in lower relief, often rather carelessly carved, conventional and repetitious. Indeed, the impression of mass-production is strong, and one can without much trouble pick out identical stock figures or groups of such. We find such stock motifs as a "man-leading-a-horse", "the chariot group", "bowmen shooting", "two soldiers marching" which are repeated as if either copied from each other or from the master craftsman's pattern-book. It was no doubt only by such wholesale organisation that the palace could be so lavishly decorated with carvings in a reasonably brief period of time. But in treatment and choice of subjects, Sennacherib makes a great step forward. The grandiose groups of large figures, fraught with majesty and symbolism, which Ashurnasirpal and, later, Sargon loved, are abandoned. The observant eye of veristic narrative, an earthier approach, is substituted, perhaps (who knows?) the result of a subtle

change of social or religious climate. The whole height of a vast stone slab, hitherto reserved for large figures, could now be used as a single "canvas" for a narrative episode, to make a lively picture, instead of being timidly cut into two by a band of irrelevant text—though this was still occasionally done in some rooms. Sargon's example is followed, of not confining a subject to one slab; instead, they run across several, to fill the whole length of a wall or fill a room, for instance, like the Siege of Lachish in Room XXXV (pls. 44–49). This records an Assyrian triumph in the South of Palestine, when in 700 B.C. Sennacherib's army swept past Jerusalem to seize this key fortress on the Egyptian frontier before setting accounts with the rebellious Hezekiah, whom Sennacherib in his annals claimed to have shut up "like a caged bird" in his stronghold of Jerusalem. The rest of the story is told in 2 Kings, 18—20, but Sennacherib's chronicles add the detail that Hezekiah bought Sennacherib off by sending timely tribute, though it may well be that the Assyrian army was content to leave the plague-ridden area at any price. Other rooms of Sennacherib's palace are carved with further episodes of this campaign in the West, occurring in Phoenicia and Palestine. Thus in the Great Hall, Slab 15 shows the flight of Luli, the king of Sidon, who fled to Tyre, and, according to Sennacherib's own words "in terror of the weapons of Ashur, my lord, he fled... to Iadnana (Cyprus) which is in the midst of the sea". We have, in this scene, only recently published,[48] the only representation, albeit damaged, of the great citadel of Tyre, with its famous Temple of Melkarth, the doorway flanked by twin free-standing pillars, prototypes of Jachin and Boaz which the Phoenician architects built for King Solomon in his Temple at Jerusalem. Another scene from Room M in the mountain landscape of Lebanon shows the capture and spoliation of a Phoenician palace, probably during the same expedition. The palace is recognisable as Phoenician by the "Tyrian windows" used for the women's quarters on the roof—windows which have a balustrade supported on little columns.[49] Other slabs from Court VI, North and East sides, teach us a little more of the fate of the prisoners from that campaign. Sennacherib, by now in his 5th campaign, describes in his annals[50] how "The people of Chaldaea, the Aramaeans, the Mannaeans, the people of the lands of Kue and Hilakku (Cilicia), Philistia and Tyre who had not submitted to my yoke, I deported and made them carry the headpad and mould bricks." In these scenes,[51] we see slaves in Phoenician and Lachishite and other dress, urged on by taskmasters under the king's watchful eye, hauling on great ropes or levers to bring up into position the great stone bull colossi or *lamassâtê* which Sennacherib has caused to be quarried from the cliff at Balatai for the gateways of this actual palace. What his father Sargon merely discussed in his letters, Sennacherib illustrates. There are interesting observations of mundane details. Two men in a coracle bring great bronze or wooden loops for the gateposts; a man draws water (no doubt to wet the ropes) from a well by means of a *shadûf*, a type of counterweighted arm still used at wells in the East; a wild sow with a row of piglets hides in the tall marsh-reeds.

The better disposed prisoners captured at Lachish were more fortunate than those conscripted to build Sennacherib's palace. We have seen that Sennacherib discards former traditional tribute and audience scenes, consisting of figures larger than life; instead, he replaced them with more ordinary themes—processions of servants leading horses,[52] carrying vases of flowers,[53] or trays of food[54]—from Room LI, or soldiers of the Royal Guard, marching behind musicians in procession before the King to the Temple of Ishtar near the palace (pl. 50).[55] Among the last may be now seen soldiers wearing the characteristic headcloth with pendant end favoured by the inhabitants of Lachish. Surely these are Lachishites enlisted into the Assyrian army (pls. 51, 53)—a practice for which, as we have mentioned, there was plenty of precedent.

As in the other palaces, so too in the "Palace without a Rival" military scenes abound. Some are routine scenes of siege and assault, but always there is present a soldier's eye for the lie of the land, which for the first time makes it possible for a background of landscape-effects to be depicted. True, mountainous terrain is still represented, as in the 9th century B. C., by a carpet of scales, but now it is spread all over the background. Trees of different type are shown, and all the varied wild life of marsh and sea. Some scenes, too, contain interesting military information. In one from the "Great Court" we have our only illustration of an Assyrian line of battle (probably in Phoenicia) moving forward behind skirmishers through lightly wooded country against a city;[56] in another, we see the army picking its way through the trackless mountains by following the river-bed, as the mountain Kurds still do today.[57]

The palace of Sennacherib was unusual in another way. It is the only palace which we know for certain was partly redecorated for use by a later ruler. Ashurbanipal, the grandson of Sennacherib, tells us in an inscription how he loved the *bît-ridûti*, or harem, where he was brought up as a child.[58] We can imagine the boy-prince, scholar and warrior under training, eagerly scanning these tales in stone of his grandfather's famous victories and mourning his murder. When he ascended the throne, he restored the *bit-riduti*, redecorated several of its rooms with magnificent sculptures illustrating his "crowning mercy" over the Elamites and Babylonians in the battle of the Ulai River in 653 B.C. (pls. 118–136) and his campaigns in Babylonia, and mercilessly sacrificed its gateway-figures his Babylonian prisoners, to the shade of his dead grandfather.

Of the art of sculpture under Esarhaddon, the son of Sennacherib, we know next to nothing. He had—or intended to have—a palace at Nimrud (the so-called South West Palace), on which he had started work, but it was never finished. Layard found in the South West corner of the mound remains of a monumental entrance, and the numerous sculptured slabs of the time of Tiglath-pileser, which Esarhaddon apparently intended to appropriate for his own residence. It is probable that the available funds and craftsmen were all engaged elsewhere. Sennacherib had decreed the destruction of Babylon, the ancient object of Assyrian hate and jealousy, and Esarhaddon, his son, finally carried it out. But Babylon, the ancient capital of culture and commerce, was so necessary to their world as to be irreplaceable, and Esarhaddon was soon reconverted to the need to rebuild it and its temples, a task lasting many years.[59]

With Ashurbanipal (668–626 B.C.), the son and successor of Esarhaddon, the art of the sculptor in ancient Mesopotamia reached its fullest and final flower. By this date, the craftsman seems to have acquired a new freedom and inspiration in depicting man and beasts, a dazzling sureness of the chisel, based not only on age-old traditions, but also on observation of life and movement, resulting in a force-fulness and precision hardly ever afterwards recaptured. We can only

speculate about the master craftsman behind these works. Was he an Assyrian, whose genius was evoked by vying with the most skilled Babylonians with whom he worked? Was he perhaps a Babylonian? A few fragments of surviving Babylonian representations of animals are of a high enough quality to support this guess.[60] Whoever this nameless genius was, the man who designed and executed Ashur-banipal's reliefs, both those showing the Ulai Battle in the "Palace without a Rival" and those we are about to describe—the war-scenes and hunting scenes in Ashurbanipal's own North palace—that man was an innovator in every direction. He can record emotion and atmosphere: individually the fleeing Elamites express their panic and excitement in lively mime (pls. 133, 135, 136); collectively, the scenes of the mad confusion of battle at the bank of the Ulai (pls. 118–127) are a masterpiece of description and atmosphere, in contrast to which, when order is restored with victory, the figures return to their ranks in neat processions of soldiers or prisoners. This ambitious concep-tion has no ancient parallel except perhaps the descriptive illustrations of the Egyptian victory over the Hittites at Kadesh depicted at Luxor, or the defeat of the Sea Peoples at Medinet Habu. Did this master-craftsman of Ashurbanipal visit Egypt in the army of Ashurbanipal when he invaded it? Or did he perhaps take part in Esarhaddon's expedition to Egypt in 667–6 B.C. and see the sack of Thebes itself? Did he at the same time draw inspiration from the great hunting scenes of Rameses depicted on the pylon wall at Medinet Habu? We cannot say.

The last series of Assyrian reliefs, to which we have just referred, was discovered in 1854 at Nineveh by Hormuzd Rassam, Layard's former assistant, and by W. K. Loftus, who took over the work from

Rassam. Rassam himself tells the story, how,[61] his finds being disappointing, his funds exhausted, his draughtsman gravely sick, and he himself under orders for home, he decided on his own responsibility to make a final gambler's throw of the dice. It happened unfortunately that an agreement existed with the French excavator, Place, whereby half the vast mound of Kuyunjik was assigned to the French, half to the British. But France had done nothing to claim her share, while the British half had been fully probed. Working secretly by night in the moonlight, Rassam and his party of workmen broke the agreement by invading the French sector. They were immediately rewarded by finding a new palace, the so-called North Palace of Ashurbanipal, containing a series of beautifully sculptured rooms, which Rassam labelled F to O, depicting Ashurbanipal's wars against Egypt, Elam, Babylon and the Arabs, all of whom were in league against him. Above all, Rassam happened on the great lion-hunting scene in Room C, a monumental record of epic scale.

The hunting scenes of Room C show a progression of events. The room is approached from a long passage (A), along one side of which the king is shown setting out with his retinue for the hunting field. These are large slabs, bearing figures three-quarters life-size. Then we enter Room C, which really represents the hunting arena; here the slabs are large, but the figures are reduced. The tale starts with the harnessing of the king's chariot to which his horses, snorting and restively pricking their ears, are led through a passage made by a double screen of canvas held up with poles by servants (pls. 57–59). The king, meanwhile, standing up in his chariot in full regalia, receives his weapons from his armourers (pl. 56). At the opposite end of an area marked off by armed guards (pl. 76), captive lions and lionesses are being released from wooden cages in which they have been confined and brought from far away. Enraged by the baying of hounds held in the leash, they rush out, only to fall beneath the pitiless shower of arrows aimed infallibly by the royal marksman, or if they survive and can outpace and leap on to his chariot, are speared from the chariot by his attendants. Of course, we are not meant to imagine as many lions as are represented, the large number depicted being the same four or five shown in successive actions, as if in a "still" film. But what are we to make of this, on the whole, slightly improbable scene of wholesale slaughter by a royal huntsman of unerring skill, dressed in such unsuitable attire? Is it simply a sort of ritual or symbolic scene (as some believe[62]), in which the king is traditionally pictured as defender of his people and their flocks against the beasts of the untamed desert? Did it really happen? Or was it merely the exaggeration and flattery suitably offered to an Oriental despot? No doubt it is best to regard it as intended magically to ensure that what ought to happen, does. Yet there is a quaint detail, which certainly seems out of place anywhere but in a record of a real, earthly event. Up a nearby hillock, tufted with pine trees and crowned by a stele commemorating a lion hunt, a crowd of Ninevite peasants are clambering to get a good view of the show (pl. 79), and we see one woman who has jostled forward too eagerly, thrust back into her proper place by her husband. In the presence of the lions there is nothing improbable. Lions of small breed certainly haunted the jungle of the Mesopotamian river marshes, and must have formed a great peril to farmers and their herds. Indeed, the last lion in Iraq was, as we have said, only killed in 1896. Ashurbanipal himself claims that they had become so numerous as to form a pest. The

Assyrian monarchs claimed often to have bagged them, and it is probable they were strictly reserved for royal sport, being captured alive and released at some convenient date for a royal sport. This is likely to have been on a festival, for we are told[63] that the god Nabu, in the course of his annual festival, goes out into the desert near Nimrud to hunt wild bulls. In this task he was no doubt imperson- ated or assisted by the king as his earthly vicar or chief huntsman, who, if he did not actually himself do the feats ascribed to him, was at least present. The deities appropriate to lion-hunting, whom Ashurbanipal mentions as aiding him, were Ashur, Nergal, Ninurta and Ishtar,[64] to whom the lion was a sacred animal.

However this may be, the total effect of this great piece of work does not seem to have quite the effect which the king who com- missioned it intended. Ashurbanipal's sculptor of genius clearly felt such a sympathy for the suffering beasts, so uselessly brave, roaring and defiant or twitching in agony of death (pls. 67–75), that he transfers our sympathy to them, instead of our feeling admiration for, and gratitude to, their executioner. The whole scene has as an epic quality to which it is impossible to find a parallel in the ancient world.

Rassam, on the expiration of his appointment by the Trustees of the British Museum, left for Aden, where he took up a consular post. In those days it was not yet possible for excavating to be considered as an independent career. Only those who possessed private means, like Schliemann, in a later generation, could pursue it continuously. Meanwhile, another British body, calling itself the Assyrian Excavation Fund, had entered the field in 1853, employing as archaeologist a geologist named William Kennett Loftus, accompa- nied by William Boutcher as his draughtsman. An agreement was reached between the Fund and the British Museum, whereby Loftus took over the excavations from Rassam at Nineveh and Nimrud; Boutcher was to make drawings of the wonderful sculpture found by Rassam, which Hodder, Rassam's artist, had been too ill to do.

There was still plenty of luck left for Loftus. Following the line of Room L, found by Rassam, one wall of which was sculptured with figures returning from another (then still undiscovered) lion-hunt (pls. 81–100), he found that the passage, after turning at a right angle, led to a building with a portico supporting the remains of an upper floor. Both ground floor and upper rooms proved to contain splendid sculptures of Ashurbanipal, the lower floor containing the most delicately carved scenes of the king wearing only a headband on his head, shooting at lions more realistically either from horseback or on foot, engaging them in hand-to-hand fight, and finally ritually sacrificing the carcasses to the patron god of the chase (pls. 83–99). Further, there are exquisite scenes of similar sort, showing the hunting of wild asses (pls. 103–4) or gazelles (pl. 102). Unfortunately, in the destruction of the palace the sculptures of the upper storey had crashed down onto the floor below, and had broken. But the chief prize remained—the famous scene of Ashurbanipal, victorious, taking his ease reclining at a banquet with his queen in an arbour, after the defeat of Teumman, king of Elam, whose severed head hangs gruesomely from the branch of one of the surrounding trees, while the captive Elamite princes wait at table (pl. 105).

Owing to an unfortunate chapter of accidents, only a part of the splendid scenes found by Rassam and Loftus are known to us today. Rassam's finds were divided between the British Museum and the Louvre. Those sent home to London safely reached their destination, but the Louvre's consignment formed part of an ill-starred convoy sent down the Tigris by raft, which was attacked by Arab robbers and sunk. Worse still, Boutcher's precious portfolio of drawings, containing the only information about most of these pieces, after being sent home to the Assyrian Excavation Fund in London in 1856, mysteriously disappeared, and has never been seen since. The premature deaths of the organising secretary of the Fund, Samuel Phillips, and of Loftus himself very shortly afterwards, completed the obliteration of the record of these finds.

Thus with Rassam and Loftus and their work in the palace of Ashurbanipal at Nineveh just over a century ago, ended the brief but brilliant age of the discovery of Assyrian palaces. With Ashurbanipal, too (668–626 B. C.), ended the era of Assyrian palace-building. With him that art had reached its grand climax. Nineveh itself and the whole mighty Assyrian empire fell soon afterwards in 612 B.C. before the combined assault of new enemies, Scythians and Medes, conjoined with the resuscitated older foe, the Babylonians. By that time Archaic Greek art and architecture was nearly fully prepared and formed to teach the world what it had learnt from the Near East.

* * *

Comparatively little is known of the decoration of buildings in Babylon in the short neo-Babylonian period which followed the fall of Assyria. Did the Neo-Babylonians continue the Assyrian practice of carving the orthostats of walls with pictorial narrative?

It does not seem so; instead, they had a different system of their own. What remains from the Ishtar Gate and elsewhere, indicates that they preferred decorating entire walls from top to bottom in the form of multi-coloured tiles, modelled in relief (pls. I–VIII), a technique familiar in Babylonia dating back at least to Cassite times where the practitioners of the art had acquired great skill and proficiency. On this background, figures of mythical or real animals are loosely shown, but nevertheless repeated in a regular pattern. The impression given is totally different from that of an Assyrian-decorated palace. There the wall decoration is closely integrated into the purposes, the *raisons d'état*, of palace and king. The Babylonian tile-decorations are just reproductions in a more permanent medium of coloured hangings, embroidered cloths, or perhaps tapestries (the celebrated *Babyloniaca hyphasmata*) or even carpets, which it is still a common custom in the East to hang on walls. The motifs on these tiles may be symbolic, propitious and apotropaic, but are in character hardly more significant than that.

Under the Persian kings (550–333 B.C.) some of the traditions of the Assyrian palace builders enjoyed a brief rebirth. But Darius and Xerxes, masters of a world empire extending from Egypt to the borders of India, meant their palaces, built by the labour of craftsmen from many subject nations, to reflect in their architecture and decoration, the varied national loyalties to which Persia claimed to be the rightful heir, expressing them in a sort of architectural *koinê* or common speech.

The Persian kings had at least two capital cities. Of one, Ekbatana, and its royal buildings, nothing has yet been excavated. The other, Susa, the former capital of the Elamites, had lain abandoned after its destruction by Ashurbanipal. The Achaemenids rebuilt it as their southern capital; but of Susa's great *apadana* little remained when it was excavated by the French. We know, however, that its roof was supported by capitals formed of kneeling bulls (pl. XIII). This is a purely Achaemenid conception as far as we at present know; but also, they took over the neo-Babylonian system of decoration with glazed tiles in relief, using figures of mythical animals loosely spaced on a textile-like background (cf. pls. VIII, IX). Indeed the neo-Babylonian and Persian animals—bulls and lions—are so much alike that it would be almost impossible to distinguish them but for the Persian device of outlining each *cloison* of different colour with a dark line. We meet again in the Persian scheme of tiled decoration, the Assyrian *lamassû* or protective gateway figures, in the form of man-sphinxes, but now they are often reduced to a simple group in low relief (pls. XIV, XV). The Persians also introduced a veristic detail in representing on the walls of coloured tiles the royal bodyguard, the famous "Immortals" or Ten Thousand, so-called because their strength was always made up to that number. This crack fighting force, which was to be so signally defeated by the Greeks at the

battle of Plataea in 480 B. C., is brought to life by the fine series of figures in the Louvre (pls. XVI–XXI) which show this brigade to have consisted of bowmen armed with a spear, wearing a long Elamite dress, embroidered all over with stars inscribed in a circle, while others bear miniature representations of a city (Susa, Persepolis or Ekbatana).[65] The difference of badge doubtless marks a different regiment.

The full scale of Achaemenid palace decoration has to be sought at Persepolis in Fars, where the Assyrian tradition of carved orthostats is revived, to depict soldiers, tributaries and court scenes of audience. But the art that results, though dignified, seems now lifeless and dead—a record of court etiquette in stone—waiting to be destroyed and supplanted forever by Greek art, as the Persian palaces were, in fact, destroyed by Alexander the Great.[66] With them, the last traditional elements of the decoration of the Assyrian palaces were finally extinguished.

NOTES

[1] Lloyd, Safar and Frankfort, "Excavations of Tell Uqair", *Journal of Near Eastern Studies*, II, 1943.

[2] *Syria*, XIX, 1930, pl. X.

[3] Tell Harmal: Frankfort, *Art and Archaelogy of the Ancient Orient* fig. 22. Khafaje, Mound D: Frankfort, p. 241, n. 28.

[4] Andrae, *Farbige Keramik aus Assur* (Berlin 1923). Bachmann, *Mitteilungen der Deutschen Orientgesellschaft*, 53.

[5] Woolley and Barnett, *Carchemish* III, pl. B. 62.

[6] von Oppenheim, *Der Tell Halaf*, frontispiece and p. 121 and pls. 41, 42.

[7] Delaporte, *Malatya*, I (Paris 1940), pl. 15.

[8] Layard, *Nineveh and Babylon*, (1853), figs. on pp. 276, 278, 284. A drawing of the mound appears opp. p. 273. The gateway figures, approached by a short tunnel, were still there when visited by the present writer in 1935.

[9] Thureau-Dangin and others, *Til Barsip* (Paris 1936). It is greatly to be regretted that the original drawings made at the time of their discovery have never been reproduced in colour.

[10] Layard, *Nineveh and Babylon*, p. 654.

[11] Campbell-Thompson and Hutchinson, *A Century of Exploration at Nineveh* (London, 1929).

[12] The kings represented are: Shalmaneser I, Mutakkil-Nusku, Tiglath-pileser I, Ashur-bel-kala, Adad-nirari II, Tukulti-Ninurta II, Ashurnasirpal II, Shalmaneser II, Adad-nirari III, Tiglath-pileser III, Sargon, Sennacherib, Ashurbanipal.

[13] *Genesis*, X.

[14] *Nineveh and its Remains*, I, p. 29 ff. For a summary account of the excavations, see R. D. Barnett, *Catalogue of the Nimrud Ivories in the British Museum*, p. 2 ff.

[15] Loud, *Revue d'Assyriologie*, XXVIII, 1936. Barnett, op. cit. p. 3.

[16] See Gadd, *The Stones of Assyria*, p. 3.

[17] See Barnett, op. cit. p. 70, note 12.

[18] Pyxis-lid, time of Tukulti-Ninurta I (1242–1206 B.C.). Andrae, *Das wiedererstandene Assur*, pl. 51b.

[19] See H. Güterbock, "Narration in Ancient Art: A Symposium". *American Journal of Archaeology*, 61, 1957, with an important discussion of these reliefs and the whole subject of narration.

[20] Gadd, *Stones of Assyria*, p. 124. See also Ludwig Schnitzler, "Die Trajanssäule und die mesopotamische Bildannalen", *Jahrbuch des Deutschen Archaeologischen Instituts*, 67, 1952.

[21] T. Sulimirski, "Les Archers à cheval et la cavallerie legère des anciens", *Revue internationale d'histoire militaire*, III. 1952, p. 452.

[22] For a convenient translation, see Luckenbill, *Ancient Records of Assyria*.

[23] They also welcomed the king at his entrance, fortifying each side.

[24] See the picture by Stubbs, reproduced in *History Today*, August 1957, p. 512.

[25] Perhaps this was the minor god NIN.AMAS.KU.GA, to whom a *hulduppu* goat was sacrificed to drive away sickness (Woolley, quoting Zimmern, *Journal of the Royal Asiatic Society*, 1926, p. 706). When Professor Mallowan in 1950 re-excavated passage P in the North West Palace, he found the skeleton of a gazelle under the pavement, doubtless from some such sacrifice (*Iraq*, 1954, p. 88).

[26] Thureau-Dangin and Dunand, op. cit.

[27] Thureau-Dangin and others, *Arslan Tash*.

[28] For the dedication, Budge & King, *Annals of the Kings of Assyria*, p. 167ff. Luckenbill, op. cit. I, pp. 536–9.

[29] King, *The Bronze Reliefs from the Gates of Shalmaneser*, (1915). Budge, *By Nile and Tigris*, II, pp. 78–9. Rassam's own account is in *Trans. Soc. Biblical Antiquities*, VII, 1882, and *Asshur and the Land of Nimrod*, p. 201ff. Budge was convinced that Rassam (or his relatives) had really found these bronze gates at Nimrud, the site of which he thought they had been privily pilfering, while claiming to be protecting it for the British Museum, and he believed that they were throwing up Balâwât as a smoke-screen. For this and other allegations, Rassam brought an action against Budge and won it. Unfortunately, however, the authorities of the British Museum supported Budge, who maintained his unjust assertions to the end.

[30] Unpublished at the time of writing.

[31] King, op. cit.

[32] The credit for pointing this out goes to H. Güterbock, op. cit. The above arrangement tallies completely with that of Güterbock. The order in which the bands are published by King is purely in chronological sequence of campaigns. For discussion of the correct arrangement, see Unger, "Die Wiederherstellung des Bronzetores von Balawat", *Mitteilungen des deutschen Arch. Instituts, Athenische Abteilung*, 45, 1920.

[33] King, op. cit.

[34] Luckenbill, op. cit. I.

[35] Loud & Altman, *Khorsabad II*, pp. 25–6. See also Place, *Ninive et l'Assyrie* (1867), III, pl. 72.

[36] *Odyssey*, 19. 565 ff.

[37] Luckenbill, op. cit. I, pp. 568, 611, 647.

[38] Sir Frank Stenton and others, *The Bayeux Tapestry*, Phaidon Press, 1957.

[39] Barnett, *Catalogue of the Nimrud Ivories in the British Museum*, pp. 11–12.

[40] See the forthcoming publication by R. D. Barnett and M. Falkner.

[41] Gadd, op. cit. pls. 9–11.

[42] City of Astartu: Smith, *Assyrian Sculptures in the British Museum*, pl. IX.

[43] Smith, op. cit. pl. XVII.

[44] Botta, *Monument de Ninive*, Paris 1849. See also Place's *Ninive et l'Assyrie* (3 vols., 1867).

[45] Luckenbill, II § 659. Cf. this passage with the "Black Stone of Esarhaddon", B. M. 91027, which evidently illustrates his version of these pictograms.

[46] Mahmud-el-Amin, "Die Reliefs mit Beischriften von Sargon II", *Sumer* IX, 1953.

[47] Waterman, *Royal Correspondence of the Assyrian Empire*, I, p. 125, II, p. 758.

[48] Barnett, *Archaeology*, July 1956, fig. p. 93, see p. 91.

[49] Layard, *Monuments of Niniveh*, 2nd series, pl. 40; Paterson, pls. 83–84. See Barnett, *Catalogue of the Nimrud Ivories*, pp. 145–7

[50] Luckenbill, II, § 383.

[51] B.M. 124820—4. Paterson, pls. 23—36: Barnett, "The Siege of Lachish", *Israel Exploration Journal*, 1958.

[52] S. Smith, *Assyrian Sculptures in the British Museum*, pls. LXV—LXVII.

[53] Unpublished.

[54] S. Smith, op. cit. pl. LXVIII.

[55] Gadd, *Stones of Assyria*, pls. 21—23.

[56] Paterson, pl. 7.

[57] Gadd, pl. 18.

[58] Luckenbill, II § 321.

[59] See Hildegard Lewy, "Nitokris-Naqia", *Journal of Near Eastern Studies*, XI, 1952.

[60] e. g., the clay lion, Jordan, *Ausgrabungen in Uruk*, 1930-1, pl. 24.

[61] *Asshur and the Land of Nimrud*, pp. 22ff.

[62] Wreszinski, *Löwenjagd im Alten Aegypten* (Leipzig 1932).

[63] Waterman, *Royal Correspondence of the Assyrian Empire*, I, p. 366.

[64] Luckenbill, op. cit. II § 1021, 1022, 1025.

[65] For this interpretation there is some evidence. A Greek dandy called Alkisthenes of Sybaris was noted for possessing a garment embroidered with Greek deities, and representations of Susa and Persepolis. See Barnett, "Oriental Influences on Archaic Greece", in *Aegean and Orient (Essays presented to Hetty Goldman)* p. 235.

[66] See E. Schmidt, *Persepolis* I (1953) and R. D. Barnett, "Persepolis", *Iraq* XIX, 1957.

ASSYRIAN RELIEFS
IN THE BRITISH MUSEUM

Frontispiece: Head of a winged lion-griffin from Susa (Persian relief from the Louvre)

PLATE NO.

1. A winged deity holding a goat and an ear of corn (Nimrud, North West Palace: doorway of Throne Room. B.M. No. 124561)
2. A winged deity holding a stag and a flowering branch (Nimrud, North West Palace: doorway of Throne Room. B.M. No. 124560)
3. Two winged goddesses, perhaps representing a form of Ishtar, holding a necklace before a Sacred Tree (Nimrud, North West Palace: Room I. B.M. No. 124581)
4. A winged monster, driven out by the god Ninurta (Nimrud, Temple of Ninurta: B.M. No. 124571)
5. A winged goddess holding a necklace: detail of 3 (Nimrud, North West Palace: Room I. B.M. No. 124581)
6. A winged deity, tending a Sacred Tree (Nimrud, North West Palace: Room Z. B.M. No. 124580)
7. Two winged eagle-headed deities magically anointing a Sacred Tree (Nimrud, North West Palace: Room I. B.M. No. 124583)
8. A winged eagle-headed deity magically anointing a Sacred Tree: detail of 7 (Nimrud, North West Palace: Room I. B.M. No. 124583)
9. Two Phoenicians, one saluting by cracking the fingers, the other bringing monkeys as gifts to the king (Nimrud, North West Palace: North Entrance, Room D. B.M. No. 124562)
10. King Ashurnasirpal leading the assault of a city, under fire of arrows (Nimrud, North West Palace: Throne Room. B.M. No. 124552)
11. A city being attacked with mines and a battering ram: continuing 10 right (Nimrud, North West Palace: Throne Room. B.M. No. 124553)
12. The assault of a city: grappling the ram: detail of 11 (Nimrud, North West Palace: Throne Room. B.M. No. 124553)
13. A Phoenician saluting by cracking the fingers (Nimrud, North West Palace: North Entrance. B.M. No. 118930)
14. King Ashurnasirpal leads his chariots, guided by the winged figure of the god Ashur: mummers mime in celebration (Nimrud, North West Palace: Throne Room. B.M. Nos. 124548, 124550)
15. King Ashurnasirpal, shooting at enemy bowmen from his chariot (Nimrud, North West Palace: Throne Room. B.M. No. 124546)
16. Assyrian troops fording a river (Nimrud, North West Palace: Throne Room. B.M. No. 124540)
17. Assyrian troops fording a river: detail of 16 (Nimrud, North West Palace: Throne Room. B.M. No. 124540)
18. Assyrian troops fording a river: continuing 16 right (Nimrud, North West Palace: Throne Room. B.M. No. 124540)
19. Assyrian troops fording a river: detail of 18 (Nimrud, North West Palace: Throne Room. B.M. No. 124540)
20. King Ashurnasirpal leading the river crossing: continuing 18 right (Nimrud, North West Palace: Throne Room. B.M. No. 124540)
21. King Ashurnasirpal's encampment and stables (Nimrud, North West Palace: Throne Room. B.M. No. 124548)
22. Fugitives under fire swimming on skin-floats to a city (Nimrud, North West Palace: Throne Room. B.M. No. 124539)
23. King Ashurnasirpal leading with fire of arrows the assault of a city which is attacked with a battering ram (Nimrud, North West Palace: Throne Room. B.M. No. 124536)
24. King Ashurnasirpal leading a chariot charge against a city (Nimrud, North West Palace: Throne Room. B.M. No. 124556)
25. King Ashurnasirpal leading a chariot charge against a city: continuing 24 right (Nimrud, North West Palace: Throne Room. B.M. No. 124555)
26. King Ashurnasirpal hunts lions from the chariot (Nimrud, North West Palace: Throne Room. B.M. No. 124534)
27. King Ashurnasirpal hunts the wild bull from

the chariot (Nimrud, North West Palace: Throne Room. B.M. No. 124553)

28. King Ashurnasirpal quaffing wine between his cup-bearer and the Keeper of his Bow (Nimrud, North West Palace: Throne Room. B.M. Nos. 124564–6)

29. King Ashurnasirpal quaffing wine (Nimrud, North West Palace: Throne Room. B.M. No. 118928)

30. Winged deity magically anointing King Ashurnasirpal's cup-bearer: continuing 28 left (Nimrud, North West Palace: Throne Room. B.M. Nos. 124564–6)

31. Winged deity magically anointing the Keeper of the King's Bow: continuing 28 right (Nimrud, North West Palace: Throne Room. B.M. Nos. 124564–6)

32. Detail from the "Black Obelisk" of Shalmaneser: wild beasts in a royal park (Nimrud. B.M. Nos. 124564–6)

33. Detail from the "Black Obelisk" of Shalmaneser: tribute-bringers (Nimrud. B.M. No. 118885)

34. Detail from the "Black Obelisk" of Shalmaneser: tribute-bringers (Nimrud. B.M. No. 118885)

35. A city, perhaps in Babylonia, stormed by King Tiglath-pileser (Nimrud, Central Palace. B.M. No. 118882)

36. Scribes counting prisoners and spoil, after the storming of a city by King Tiglath-pileser: continuing 35 right (Nimrud, Central Palace. B.M. No. 118882)

37. Cattle captured by King Tiglath-pileser (Nimrud, Central Palace. B.M. No. 118881)

38. Storming a city with battering-rams, probably in Babylonia: King Tiglath-pileser (Nimrud, Central Palace. B.M. No. 118903)

39. Beduin Arab woman with camels, asking mercy of King Tiglath-pileser (Nimrud, Central Palace. B.M. No. 118901)

40/41. King Tiglath-pileser leading the storming of a city, probably in Babylonia: prisoners beheaded and impaled (Nimrud, Central Palace. B.M. No. 118903)

42. Head of a tributary (Khorsabad, Palace of Sargon. B.M. No. 118828)

43. A tributary with horses (Khorsabad, Palace of Sargon. B.M. No. 118828)

44. The siege of Lachish: part of the siege mound, and prisoners marched out from the city (Nineveh, Palace of Sennacherib: Room XXXV. B.M. No. 124907)

45. The siege of Lachish: prisoners marched out from the city: continuing 44 right (Nineveh, Palace of Sennacherib: Room XXXV. B.M. No. 124907)

46. The siege of Lachish: prisoners flayed alive (Nineveh, Palace of Sennacherib: Room XXXV. B.M. No. 124908)

47. The siege of Lachish: Hebrew prisoners imploring mercy from Sennacherib, who sits enthroned (Nineveh, Palace of Sennacherib: Room XXXV. B.M. No. 124909)

48. The siege of Lachish: Hebrew prisoners imploring mercy: detail of 47 (Nineveh, Palace of Sennacherib: Room XXXV. B.M. No. 124909)

49. The siege of Lachish: Hebrew prisoners imploring mercy: continuing 47 left (Nineveh, Palace of Sennacherib: Room XXXV. B.M. No. 124909)

50. Musicians leading a religious procession to the Temple of Ishtar (Nineveh, Palace of Sennacherib: Room XXXV. B.M. No. 124948)

51. Assyrian soldiers (of Philistine or Lachish regiment) in procession to the temple of Ishtar (Nineveh, Palace of Sennacherib. B.M. No. 124951)

52. Head, perhaps from a cult-statue (Nineveh, B.M. No. 118908)

53. Assyrian soldiers (of Philistine or Lachish regiment) in procession to the temple of Ishtar (Nineveh, Palace of Sennacherib. B.M. No. 124901)

54. Eunuch musician with tame lion and priestess, in a royal park (Nineveh, Palace of Ashurbanipal: Room E. B.M. No. 118916)

55. Lion and lioness in the royal park (Nineveh, Palace of Ashurbanipal: Room E. B.M. No. 118914)

56. Fletchers and bowyers testing King Ashurbanipal's weapons (Nineveh, Palace of Ashurbanipal: Room C. B.M. No. 124884)

57. King Ashurbanipal's horses led to his chariot for the lion hunt (Nineveh, Palace of Ashurbanipal: Room C. B.M. No. 124858)

58. King Ashurbanipal's horses led to his chariot for the lion hunt: continuing 57

(Nineveh, Palace of Ashurbanipal: Room C. B.M. No. 124860)

59. King Ashurbanipal's horses being harnessed for the lion hunt (Nineveh, Palace of Ashurbanipal: Room C. B.M. No. 124859)

60. The lion hunt: King Ashurbanipal slaying a lion from his chariot (Nineveh, Palace of Ashurbanipal: Room C. B.M. No. 124854)

61. The lion hunt: King Ashurbanipal slaying a lion from his chariot (Nineveh, Palace of Ashurbanipal: Room C. B.M. No. 124850)

62. The lion hunt: King Ashurbanipal slaying a lion from his chariot (Nineveh, Palace of Ashurbanipal: Room C. B.M. No. 124867)

63. The lion hunt: King Ashurbanipal shooting at lions from his chariot (Nineveh, Palace of Ashurbanipal: Room C. B.M. No. 124867)

64. The lion hunt: a horse's head (Nineveh, Palace of Ashurbanipal: Room C)

65. The lion hunt: King Ashurbanipal: detail of 63 (Nineveh, Palace of Ashurbanipal: Room C. B.M. No. 124867)

66. Lion in its cage, ready for the hunt (Nineveh, Palace of Ashurbanipal: Room C. B.M. No. 124883)

67. The lion hunt: a wounded lion (Nineveh, Palace of Ashurbanipal: Room C. B.M. No. 124857)

68. The lion hunt: a dead lion (Nineveh, Palace of Ashurbanipal: Room C. B.M. No. 124855)

69. The lion hunt: a wounded lion (Nineveh,

Palace of Ashurbanipal: Room C. B.M. No. 124852)

70. The lion hunt: wounded lions (Nineveh, Palace of Ashurbanipal: Room C. B.M. No. 124868)

71. The lion hunt: a wounded lioness (Nineveh, Palace of Ashurbanipal: Room C. B.M. No. 124856)

72. The lion hunt: dead lions and a lioness (Nineveh, Palace of Ashurbanipal: Room C. B.M. No. 124868)

73. The lion hunt: a wounded lion: continuing 74 right (Nineveh, Palace of Ashurbanipal: Room C. B.M. No. 124869)

74. The lion hunt: wounded lion: continuing 73 left (Nineveh, Palace of Ashurbanipal: Room C. B.M. No. 124864)

75. The lion hunt: a dead lion (Nineveh, Palace of Ashurbanipal: Room C. B.M. No. 124856)

76/77. The lion hunt: the line of guards at the edge of the arena (Nineveh, Palace of Ashurbanipal: Room C. B.M. No. 124860)

78. The lion hunt: servants carrying home a dead lion (Nineveh, Palace of Ashurbanipal: Room C. B.M. No. 124885)

79. Spectators of the lion hunt climbing a wooded knoll, surmounted by a stele (Nineveh, Palace of Ashurbanipal: Room C. B.M. No. 124862)

80. Spectators of the lion hunt climbing a wooded knoll, surmounted by a stele: detail of 79 (Nineveh, Palace of Ashurbanipal: Room C. B.M. No. 124862)

81. Hounds led home after the lion hunt (Nineveh, Palace of Ashurbanipal: Room R. B.M. 124893)

82. Servants bringing home a lion's carcass (Nineveh, Palace of Ashurbanipal: Room R. B.M. No. 124890)

83. King Ashurbanipal shooting at lions from the saddle (Nineveh, Palace of Ashurbanipal: Room S. B.M. No. 124875)

84. King Ashurbanipal shooting at lions from the saddle: detail of 83. (Nineveh, Palace of Ashurbanipal: Room S. B.M. No. 124875)

85. The lion hunt: one of King Ashurbanipal's beaters, dismounted (Nineveh, Palace of Ashurbanipal: Room S. B.M. No. 124875)

86. The lion hunt: a lion takes the first arrow (Nineveh, Palace of Ashurbanipal: Room S. B.M. No. 124877)

87. King Ashurbanipal's horse saddled and ready for the lion hunt (Nineveh, Palace of Ashurbanipal: Room S. B.M. No. 124882)

88. King Ashurbanipal testing his bows and arrows offered by his servants (Nineveh, Palace of Ashurbanipal: Room S. B.M. No. 124878)

89. The lion hunt: King Ashurbanipal spearing a lion from the saddle (Nineveh, Palace of Ashurbanipal: Room S. B.M. No. 124875)

90. King Ashurbanipal slaying and sacrificing lions—in three friezes (Nineveh, Palace of Ashurbanipal: Room S. B.M. Nos. 124886/7)

91. The lion hunt: King Ashurbanipal shooting at a leaping lion: detail of 90, top frieze

29

92. The lion hunt: King Ashurbanipal shooting at a leaping lion, with another following: detail of 90, top frieze, and continuing 91 right (Nineveh, Palace of Ashurbanipal: Room S. B.M. Nos. 124886/7).

93. The lion hunt: the lion released from the cage: detail of 90, top frieze, and continuing 92 right (Nineveh, Palace of Ashurbanipal: Room S. B.M. Nos. 124886/7).

94. The lion hunt: King Ashurbanipal twisting the lion's tail: detail of 90, centre frieze (Nineveh, Palace of Ashurbanipal: Room S. B.M. Nos. 124886/7).

95. The lion hunt: the beater whipping up a lion: detail of 90, centre frieze, and continuing 94 right (Nineveh, Palace of Ashurbanipal: Room S. B.M. Nos. 124886/7).

96. The lion hunt: King Ashurbanipal's chariot at attention: detail of 90, centre frieze, and continuing 95 right (Nineveh, Palace of Ashurbanipal: Room S. B.M. Nos. 124886/7).

97. The lion hunt: King Ashurbanipal making a libation over the slain lions: detail of 90, lower frieze, and continuing 95 right, 96 left (Nineveh, Palace of Ashurbanipal: Room S. B.M. Nos. 124886/7).

98. Musicians performing during the rituals after the lion hunt: detail of 90, lower frieze, and continuing 97 left (Nineveh, Palace of Ashurbanipal: Room S. B.M. Nos. 124886/7).

99. The lion hunt: riding horses standing by, becoming restive: detail of 90, lower frieze, and continuing 97 right (Nineveh, Palace of Ashurbanipal: Room S. B.M. Nos. 124886/7).

100. The lion hunt: servants conversing over the slain lions (Nineveh, Palace of Ashurbanipal: Room S. B.M. No. 124877).

101. The stag hunt: stags and deer caught in nets (Nineveh, Palace of Ashurbanipal: Room S. B.M. No. 124871).

102. A herd of gazelle (Nineveh, Palace of Ashurbanipal: Room S. B.M. No. 124874).

103. Hunting wild ass: the herd in flight (Nineveh, Palace of Ashurbanipal: Room S. B.M. No. 124877).

104. A wild ass lassoed (Nineveh, Palace of Ashurbanipal: Room S. B.M. No. 124882).

105. King Ashurbanipal banqueting in an arbour with his Queen (Nineveh, Palace of Ashurbanipal: the upper room above Room S. B.M. No. 124920).

106. Attendants bringing food and drink for King Ashurbanipal's banquet in the arbour (Nineveh, Palace of Ashurbanipal: the upper room above Room S. B.M. No. 124916).

107. Musicians playing for King Ashurbanipal's banquet in the arbour (Nineveh, Palace of Ashurbanipal: the upper room above Room S. B.M. No. 124922).

108. War against the Arabs: pursued by Assyrian cavalry, an Arab falls from his camel (Nineveh, Palace of Ashurbanipal: Room L. B.M. No. 124926).

109. War against the Arabs: an Arab at the point of a spear: fleeing Arabs turn to shoot back at pursuing Assyrians (Nineveh, Palace of Ashurbanipal: Room L. B.M. No. 124926).

110. War against the Arabs: two Arabs on a camel, pursued by Assyrian archers and spearmen: detail of part of 113 (Nineveh, Palace of Ashurbanipal: Room L. B.M. No. 124926).

111. War against the Arabs: an Arab slain by an Assyrian spearman: fleeing Arabs on a camel pursued by Assyrian cavalry (Nineveh, Palace of Ashurbanipal: Room L. B.M. No. 124926).

112. War against the Arabs: two Arabs on a camel, pursued by Assyrian cavalry (Nineveh, Palace of Ashurbanipal: Room L. B.M. No. 124926).

113. War against the Arabs: fleeing Arabs pursued by Assyrian cavalry: continuing 112 right (Nineveh, Palace of Ashurbanipal: Room L. B.M. No. 124926).

114. An Arab tent burning (Nineveh, Palace of Ashurbanipal: Room L. B.M. No. 124927).

115. War against the Arabs: Arabs falling from a camel (Nineveh, Palace of Ashurbanipal: Room L. B.M. No. 124926).

116. Arab fleeing wounded on a camel (Nineveh, Palace of Ashurbanipal: Room L. B.M. No. 124927).

117. The capture of the Elamite King, Ummanaldash (Nineveh, Palace of Ashurbanipal. B.M. No. 124793).

118. Ashurbanipal's defeat of the Elamites at the

river Ulai (Nineveh, Palace of Sennacherib: Room XXXIII. B.M. No. 124801)

119. The defeat of the Elamites at the river Ulai: continuing 118 left (Nineveh, Palace of Sennacherib: Room XXXIII. B.M. No. 124801)

120. The defeat of the Elamites at the river Ulai: detail of 118 (Nineveh, Palace of Sennacherib: Room XXXIII. B.M. No. 124801)

121. The defeat of the Elamites at the river Ulai: an Elamite prince falling from his chariot: detail of 119 (Nineveh, Palace of Sennacherib: Room XXXIII. B.M. No. 124801)

122. The battle against the Elamites at the river Ulai: detail of 119. (Nineveh, Palace of Sennacherib: Room XXXIII. B.M. No. 124801)

123. The defeat of the Elamites at the river Ulai: an Elamite, imploring an Assyrian soldier to end his life: detail of 119 (Nineveh, Palace of Sennacherib: Room XXXIII. B.M. No. 124801)

124. The defeat of the Elamites at the river Ulai: Elamite dead: detail of 118 (Nineveh, Palace of Sennacherib: Room XXXIII. B.M. No. 124801)

125. The defeat of the Elamites at the river Ulai: detail of 118 (Nineveh, Palace of Sennacherib: Room XXXIII. B.M. No. 124801)

126. The defeat of the Elamites at the river Ulai: Elamite archers fighting in retreat (Nineveh, Palace of Sennacherib: Room XXXIII. B.M. No. 124801)

127. The defeat of the Elamites at the river Ulai: Elamite horsemen trying to escape (Nineveh, Palace of Sennacherib: Room XXXIII. B.M. No. 124801)

128. An Assyrian slaying Ituni, an Elamite officer (Nineveh, Palace of Ashurbanipal: Room I. B.M. No. 128941)

129. Assyrian chariots driving Elamite prisoners home after the defeat of the Elamites at the river Ulai (Nineveh, Palace of Sennacherib: Room XXXIII. B.M. No. 124802)

130. Executing Elamites (Nineveh, Palace of Sennacherib: Room XXXIII. B.M. No. 124801)

131. Assyrians counting Elamite heads (Nineveh, Palace of Sennacherib: Room XXXIII. B.M. No. 124801)

132. Assyrians demolishing the town Hamanu (Nineveh, Palace of Ashurbanipal: upper room above Room S. B.M. No. 124919)

133. Above: a pavilion in a well-watered park, perhaps Babylon. Below: fleeing Elamites (Nineveh, Palace of Ashurbanipal: Room H. B.M. No. 124939)

134. A pavilion in a well-watered park, perhaps Babylon: detail of 133 (Nineveh, Palace of Ashurbanipal: Room H. B.M. No. 124939)

135. Fleeing Elamites: detail of 133 (Nineveh, Palace of Ashurbanipal: Room H. B.M. No. 124939)

136. Above: a triple-walled city. Below: fleeing Elamites (Nineveh, Palace of Ashurbanipal: Room I. B.M. No. 124938)

THE BRONZE GATES OF SHALMANESER FROM IMGÛR-BÊL (BALÂWÂT) IN THE BRITISH MUSEUM

Note: Pl. 138 and 139 show the complete gates. The decorative bands are keyed from top to bottom: a-l, m-x, captions following the bands from left to right. Pl. 137 and 140–173 show details of the gates and here the bands are keyed both in relation to each other and to the pictures of the complete gates. // denotes end of band.

PLATE NO.

137. *a)* Assyrian cavalry attacking Parga (854 B.C.) (Band a: // left of 140a)
b) Assyrians cutting down fruit trees at Qarqar (854 B.C.) (Band b: // left of 140b)
c) Assyrians in the march to the source of the Tigris (853 B.C.) (Band c: // left of 140c)
d) Shalmaneser receiving the news of the surrender of the city of Kulîsî (853 B.C.) (Band d: // left of 140d)

138. The bronze gates of Shalmaneser from Imgûr-Bêl (Balâwât): left-hand gate
a) The attack on Parga: the assault on Ada in Hamath (854 B.C.)
b) Spoil from Qarqar brought before Shalmaneser enthroned (854 B.C.)
c) The march to the source of the Tigris: a chief's submission: Shalmaneser's expedi-

31

tion sacrificing at the source of the Tigris (853 B.C.)

d) Slaughter of the men of Kulîsî: Shalmaneser's expedition to the source of the Tigris: sacrifices (853 B.C.)

e) Slaughter of the Urartians of the Urartian capital, Arzashkûn: burning of Arzashkûn (857 B.C.)

f) Tribute of horses and cattle from Gilzanî: the Assyrian army marching to Gilzanî (857 B.C.)

g) The attack and siege of Arnê, capital of Bît-Agûsî in North Syria (850 B.C.)

h) Captured Syrians and Syrian flocks (campaign of 850 B.C.): assault of cities of Bît-Agûsî

i) Tribute of the King of Unki (Orontes Valley 858 B.C.) and the embassy offering his daughter to Shalmaneser in marriage

j) Tribute and embassy of the King of Unki (Orontes Valley 858 B.C.)

k) Tribute of the kingdom of Carchemish on the Euphrates (858 B.C.)

l) Tribute of the kingdom of Carchemish on the Euphrates (858 B.C.)

139. The bronze gates of Shalmaneser from Imgûr-Bêl (Balâwât): right-hand gate

m) Tribute of the city of Tyre (Phoenician campaign 859 B.C.)

n) The assault on the city of Hazazu (859 B.C.)

o) The assault on Dabigu, capital of Bît-Adini in N. E. Syria (858 B.C.)

p) The assault on Dabigu, capital of Bît-Adini in N. E. Syria (858 B.C.): prisoners

q) Shalmaneser receiving the submission of Adini, chief of Bît Dakuri, a Chaldaean tribe in South Mesopotamia (851 B.C.): tribute of the Dakurians

r) Tribute of the Chaldaeans (851 B.C.)

s) The sack of an Urartian city: Urartian prisoners (860 B.C.)

t) The attack on an Urartian city: Urartian prisoners (860 B.C.)

u) The attack on Ashtamaku, capital of the kingdom of Hamath (849 B.C.)

v) Assyrians marching against Hamath: captives from a city of Hamath (849 B.C.)

w) Shalmaneser setting up his image by Lake Van: Assyrian troops crossing the Urartian mountains (860 B.C.)

x) The assault on the city of Sugunia: Urartian captives from Sugunia (860 B.C.)

140. a) The Assyrian archers giving covering fire to a battering-ram, attacking Parga (854 B.C.) (Band a: right of 139a, left of 141a)

b) The city of Qarqar captured (854 B.C.) Band b: right of 139b, left of 141b)

c) Assyrian chariots in the march to the source of the Tigris (853 B.C.) (Band c: right of 139c, left of 141c)

d) Assyrians slaying the men of Kulîsî: Shalmaneser receiving the news of the surrender of the city (853 B.C.) (Band d: right of 139d)

141. a) Archers attacking Parga: the Assyrians' fortified camp: the army assaulting Ada in Hamath (see 142a) (854 B.C.) (Band a: right of 140a, left of 142a)

b) Spoil from Qarqar, brought before Shalmaneser enthroned (see 142b) (854 B.C.) (Band b: right of 140b, left of 142b)

c) Shalmaneser receiving a chief's submission on the expedition to the source of the Tigris, escorted by chariots (see 142c) (853 B.C.) (Band c: right of 140c, left of 142c)

142. a) The army assaulting Ada in Hamath (854 B.C.) (Band a: right of 141a, left of 145a)

b) Spoil from Qarqar brought before Shalmaneser enthroned (854 B.C.) (Band b: right of 141b, left of 145b)

c) Chariots escorting Shalmaneser to receive a chief's submission on the expedition to the source of the Tigris (see 141c): Shalmaneser's expedition sacrificing at the source of the Tigris (853 B.C.) (Band c: right of 141c and 143a, left of 145c)

143. a) Shalmaneser receiving a chief's submission on the expedition to the source of the Tigris (853 B.C.) (Band c: left of 142c)

b) Shalmaneser's expedition to the source of the Tigris (853 B.C.) (Band d: left of 144b)

c) The slaughter of the Urartians of the Urartian capital, Arzashkûn (857 B.C.) (Band e: left of 144c)

144. a) Chariots escorting Shalmaneser to receive a chief's submission on the expedition to the source of the Tigris (see 141c): Shalmaneser's expedition sacrificing at the source of the

Tigris (853 B.C.) (Band c: right of 141c and 143a, left of 145c)

b) Sacrifices at the source of the Tigris (853 B.C.) (Band d: right of 143b, left of 145d)

c) Slaughter of Urartians of the city of Arzashkûn (857 B.C.) (Band e: right of 143c, left of 145e)

145. a) Assault on Ada in Hamath (854 B.C.) (Band a: right of 142a //)

b) Right: an Assyrian camp (Band b: right of 142b //)

c) Sacrifices at the source of the Tigris (853 B.C.) (Band c: right of 142c, and 144a //)

d) Sacrifices at the source of the Tigris before the River Gods (853 B.C.) (Band d: right of 144b //)

e) Slaughter of the Urartians of the city Arzashkûn (857 B.C.) (Band e: right of 144c //)

146. a) Slaughter of Urartians (857 B.C.) (Band e: // left of 147b)

b) Tribute of cattle from Gilzanî (857 B.C.) (Band f: // left of 147c)

c) Chariots attacking Arnê (850 B.C.) (Band g: // left of 147d)

d) Chariots and captive Syrians (850 B.C.) (Band h: // left of 147e)

147. a) Execution of the men of Kulîsî (853 B.C.) (Band d: right of 139a)

b) Burning of Arzashkûn (857 B.C.) (Band e: right of 146a)

c) Tribute of horses from Gilzanî (857 B.C.) (Band f: right of 146b, left of 148a)

d) Chariots attacking Arnê, capital of Bît-Agûsî in North Syria (850 B.C.) (Band g: right of 146c, left of 148b)

148. a) Tribute of Gilzanî (857 B.C.) (Band f: right of 147c, left of 149a)

b) Siege of Arnê (850 B.C.) (Band g: right of 147d, left of 149b)

c) Conquest of another city of Bît-Agûsî (850 B.C.) (Band h: right of 147d, left of 149c)

149. a) Tribute of Gilzanî (857 B.C.) (Band f: right of 148a)

b) Siege of Arnê (850 B.C.) (Band g: right of 148b)

c) Conquest of another city of Bît-Agûsî (850 B.C.) (Band h: right of 148c)

150. a) Slaughter of the Urartians of the city Arzashkûn (857 B.C.) (Band e: right of 144c //)

b) The Assyrian army advancing to Gilzanî from its camp (857 B.C.) (Band f: right of 149a //)

c) The Assyrian camp before Arnê (850 B.C.) (Band g: right of 149b //)

d) Assault of cities of Bît-Agûsî (850 B.C.) (Band h: right of 149c //)

151. a) Tribute of the King of Unki (Orontes Valley) (858 B.C.) (Band i: // left of 152a)

b) Tribute of the King of Unki (Orontes Valley) (858 B.C.) (Band j: // left of 152b)

c) Tribute of the kingdom of Carchemish on the Euphrates (858 B.C.) (Band k: // left of 152c)

d) Tribute of the kingdom of Carchemish on the Euphrates (858 B.C.) (Band l: // left of 152d)

152. a) Tribute of the King of Unki (Orontes Valley) (858 B.C.) (Band i: right of 151a)

b) Tribute of the King of Unki (Orontes Valley) (858 B.C.) (Band j: right of 151b, left of 153a)

c) Tribute of the kingdom of Carchemish on the Euphrates (858 B.C.) (Band k: right of 151c, left of 153b)

d) Tribute of the kingdom of Carchemish on the Euphrates (858 B.C.) (Band l: right of 151d, left of 153c)

153. a) The embassy of the King of Unki (Orontes Valley) (858 B.C.), offering his daughter to Shalmaneser in marriage (Band j: right of 152b, left of 154b)

b) Tribute of the kingdom of Carchemish on the Euphrates (858 B.C.) (Band k: right of 152c, left of 154a)

c) Tribute of the kingdom of Carchemish on the Euphrates (858 B.C.) (Band l: right of 152d, left of 154b)

154. a) Assyrians receiving the tribute of the kingdom of Carchemish on the Euphrates: the royal tent (858 B.C.) (Band k: right of 153b, left of 155c)

b) Assyrians receiving the tribute of the kingdom of Carchemish on the Euphrates (858 B.C.) (Band l: right of 153d)

155. a) Assyrians receiving the embassy of the King of Unki (858 B.C.) (Band i: left of 156a)

b) Assyrians receiving the embassy of the King of Unki: the royal tent (858 B.C.) (Band j: right of 159a, left of 156b)

c) Assyrians receiving the tribute of the kingdom of Carchemish on the Euphrates: the royal tent (858 B.C.) (Band k: right of 154b, left of 156c)

156. *a)* Assyrians receiving the tribute of the King of Unki (Orontes Valley): the city is on an island reached from the Assyrian camp by boat (858 B.C.) (Band i: right of 155a //)

b) Assyrians leaving camp receiving the tribute of the King of Unki (Orontes Valley) (858 B.C.) (Band j: right of 155b //)

c) Assyrians receiving the tribute of the kingdom of Carchemish on the Euphrates (858 B.C.) (Band k: right of 155c)

d) Assyrians leaving camp receiving the tribute of the kingdom of Carchemish on the Euphrates (858 B.C.) (Band l: //)

157. *a)* Tribute of the city of Tyre (Phoenician campaign 859 B.C.) (Band m: // left of 158a)

b) The assault on the city of Hazazu (859 B.C.) from the Assyrian camp: chariots escorting Shalmaneser (Band n: // left of 158b)

c) The assault on Dabigu, capital of Bît-Adini in North-east Syria (858 B.C.) (Band o: // left of 158c)

158. *a)* Shalmaneser receiving the tribute of the city of Tyre (Phoenician campaign 859 B.C.) (Band m: right of 157a, left of 159a)

b) The assault on the city of Hazazu (859 B.C.) from the Assyrian camp: Shalmaneser receiving prisoners (Band n: right of 157b, left of 159b)

c) The assault on Dabigu, capital of Bît-Adini in North-east Syria: Shalmaneser enthroned (858 B.C.) (Band o: right of 157c, left of 159c)

159. *a)* Archers and chariots escorting Shalmaneser to receive the tribute of the city of Tyre (Phoenician campaign 859 B.C.) (Band m: right of 158a, left of 160a)

b) Assault on the city of Hazazu (859 B.C.) from the Assyrian camp: prisoners (Band n: right of 158b, left of 160b)

c) Assault on Dabigu, capital of Bît-Adini in North-east Syria (858 B.C.) (Band o: right of 158c, left of 160c)

d) Assault on a Syrian city: prisoners impaled (Band p: right of 162a, left of 160d)

e) Shalmaneser advancing to receive the submission of Adini, chief of Bît Dakuri, a Chaldaean tribe in South Mesopotamia (851 B.C.) (Band q: right of 162b)

160. *a)* Assyrian chariots escorting Shalmaneser to receive the tribute of the city of Tyre (Phoenician campaign 859 B.C.) (Band m: right of 159a, left of 164a)

b) Assault on the city of Hazazu (859 B.C.) from the Assyrian camp: prisoners (Band n: right of 159b, left of 164b)

c) Assault on Dabigu, capital of Bît-Adini in North-east Syria (858 B.C.) (Band o: right of 159c, left of 164c)

161. *a)* Assyrian chariots advancing from camp against Dabigu, capital of Bît-Adini in North-east Syria (858 B.C.) (Band p: // left of 162a)

b) Shalmaneser advancing to receive the submission of Adini, chief of Bît Dakuri, a Chaldaean tribe in South Mesopotamia (851 B.C.) (Band q: // left of 162b)

c) Assyrians advancing to receive the tribute of the Chaldaeans (851 B.C.) (Band r.: // left of 162c)

162. *a)* Assault on Dabigu, capital of Bît-Adini in North-east Syria (858 B.C.) with battering ram and mines: prisoners impaled (Band p: right of 161a, left of 163b)

b) Shalmaneser receiving the submission of Adini, chief of Bît Dakuri, a Chaldaean tribe in South Mesopotamia (851 B.C.) (Band q: right of 161b, left of 163c)

c) Assyrian chariotry crossing a pontoon bridge over a river (851 B.C.) (Band r: right of 161c, left of 163d)

163. *a)* Assault on Dabigu, capital of Bît-Adini in North-east Syria (858 B.C.) (Band o: right of 158c, left of 160c)

b) Assault on Dabigu, capital of Bît-Adini in North-east Syria (858 B.C.): prisoners impaled (Band p: right of 161a and 162a)

c) Shalmaneser receiving the submission of Adini, chief of Bît Dakuri, a Chaldaean tribe in South Mesopotamia (851 B.C.) (Band q: right of 162b, left of 165a)

d) Assyrians advancing to receive the tribute

of the Chaldaeans (851 B.C.) (Band r: right of 162c, left of 165b)

164. *a)* Assyrian chariotry escorting Shalmaneser to receive the tribute of the city of Tyre (Phoenician campaign 859 B.C.) (Band m: right of 160a //)

b) Assault on the city of Hazazu (859 B.C.): the enemy butchered (Band n: right of 160b //)

c) Assault on Dabigu, capital of Bît-Adini in North-east Syria (858 B.C.) (Band o: right of 160c //)

d) Assault on Dabigu, capital of Bît-Adini in North-east Syria (858 B.C.): prisoners and a pack-mule (Band p: right of 160d //)

165. *a)* Dakurians bringing tribute through the river in boats (851 B.C.) (Band q: right of 163c, left of 166c)

b) Tribute of Chaldaeans: Shalmaneser enthroned (Band r: right of 163d, left of 166b)

c) Urartian prisoners butchered (860 B.C.) (Band s: right of 169a, left of 166c)

d) Urartian prisoners (860 B.C.) (Band t: right of 169b)

166. *a)* Dakurians bringing tribute from a city (851 B.C.) (Band q: right of 165a //)

b) Tribute of Chaldaeans, crossing a river by pontoon bridge (851 B.C.) (Band r: right of 165b //)

c) Urartians fighting (860 B.C.) (Band s: right of 165c //)

167. *a)* An Urartian city sacked (860 B.C.): a great wine-jar carried off: trees cut down: men impaled (Band s: // left of 168a)

b) Assyrian cavalry and chariots attacking an Urartian city (860 B.C.) (Band t: // left of 168b)

c) Assyrian chariotry attacking Ashtamaku, capital of the kingdom of Hamath (849 B.C.) (Band u: // left of 168c)

168. *a)* An Urartian city sacked (860 B.C.) (Band s: right of 167a: left of 169a)

b) Assyrian archers attacking an Urartian city (860 B.C.) (Band t: right of 167b, left of 169b)

c) Assyrian attacking Ashtamaku, capital of the kingdom of Hamath (849 B.C.) (Band u: right of 167c, left of 169c)

169. *a)* An Urartian city sacked (860 B.C.) (Band s: right of 168a, left of 165c)

b) Assyrians attacking and burning an Urartian city (860 B.C.) (Band t: right of 168b, left of 165d)

c) Assyrian chariots attacking Ashtamaku, capital of the kingdom of Hamath (849 B.C.) (Band u: right of 168c, left of 172a)

d) Captives from a city of Hamath (849 B.C.) (Band v: right of 171a, left of 172b)

170. *a)* Assyrian chariots marching against Hamath (849 B.C.) (Band v: // left of 171a)

b) Shalmaneser setting up his image by Lake Van (860 B.C.) (Band w: // left of 171b)

c) Assyrian chariots marching against the city of Sugunia: the Assyrian camp (860 B.C.,) (Band x: // left of 171c)

171. *a)* Assyrians marching against Hamath: captives from a city of Hamath (849 B.C.) (Band v: right of 170a, left of 172b)

b) Assyrian troops crossing the Armenian mountains to dedicate Shalmaneser's image (860 B.C.) (Band w: right of 170b, left of 172c)

c) Assault on the city of Sugunia (860 B.C.) (Band x: right of 170c, left of 172d)

172. *a)* Assault on Ashtamaku, capital of the kingdom of Hamath (849 B.C.) (Band u: right of 169c, left of 173b)

b) Captives from a city of Hamath (849 B.C.) (Band v: right of 171a, left of 173c)

c) Assyrian chariots crossing the Urartian mountains to dedicate Shalmaneser's image (860 B.C.) (Band w: right of 171b, left of 173d)

d) Assault on the city of Sugunia (860 B.C.) (Band x: right of 171c, left of 173e)

173. *a)* Assault of a city of Hamath (849 B.C.) (Band u: right of 172a //)

b) Women prisoners from a city of Hamath (849 B.C.) (Band v: right of 172b)

c) Assyrian chariots and cavalry of the royal guard (860 B.C.) (Band w: right of 172c //)

d) Yoked Urartian captives from Sugunia (860 B.C.) (Band x: right of 172d //)

NEO-BABYLONIAN RELIEFS IN THE STAATLICHE MUSEEN, BERLIN

COLOUR PLATE NO.

I. The Ishtar-Gate of Babylon: Nebuchadnezzar II (c. 570 B.C.). Coloured and glazed tiles: height 23.5 m.

II. The Ishtar-Gate of Babylon: Nebuchadnezzar II (c. 570 B.C.): another view

III. The Ishtar-Gate of Babylon: Nebuchadnezzar II (c. 570 B.C.): detail

IV. The Ishtar-Gate of Babylon: Nebuchadnezzar II (c. 570 B.C.): detail

V. Detail of ornament from the Throne Room of Nebuchadnezzar II (c. 570 B.C.) Coloured and glazed tiles: height of detail 350 cm.

VI. Part of the Procession of Lions from the Processional Way, Babylon. Coloured and glazed tiles: figure of lion about 2 m. long

VII. Lion's head: detail of ornament of the walls of the Processional Way, Babylon (c. 570 B.C.)

VIII. Bull's head: detail from the Ishtar-Gate of Babylon: Nebuchadnezzar II (c. 570 B.C.) Coloured and glazed tiles

PERSIAN RELIEFS IN THE LOUVRE

COLOUR PLATE NO.

IX. Part of the procession of lions from the "apadana" or Audience Hall of Artaxerxes Mnemon (405–362 B.C.) at Susa. Coloured and glazed tiles: breadth 3 m. 60

X. Head of a lion: the procession of lions from the "apadana" or Audience Hall of Artaxerxes Mnemon (405–362 B.C.) at Susa

XI. Winged bull from a decorative frieze at Susa. Coloured and glazed tiles: height 1 m. 40

XII. Winged bull from a decorative frieze at Susa: detail of XI

XIII. Column-capital in the form of volutes supporting double protomes of bulls, from the "apadana" or Audience Hall of Artaxerxes Mnemon (405–362 B.C.) at Susa. Grey marble: height 5 m. 80

XIV. A procession of winged lion-griffins: part of a frieze from Susa. Coloured and glazed tiles: height 1 m. 40

XV. Head of a winged lion-griffin: part of a frieze from Susa

XVI. A parade of the Persian Royal Guard: part of a frieze from the Palace of Darius I at Susa (c. 490 B.C.)

XVII. Head of one of the Persian Royal Guard: detail of XVI.: part of a frieze from the Palace of Darius I at Susa (c. 490 B.C.)

XVIII. Head of one of the Persian Royal Guard: detail of XVI.: part of a frieze from the Palace of Darius I at Susa (c. 490 B.C.)

XIX. A parade of the Persian Royal Guard: another part of the frieze from the Palace of Darius I at Susa (c. 490 B.C.). Coloured and glazed tiles: height 1 m. 47

XX. A member of the Persian Royal Guard: detail from another part of the frieze from the Palace of Darius I at Susa (c. 490 B.C.).

XXI. The Persian Royal Guard: detail from XVI in the Palace of Darius I at Susa (c. 490 B.C.) Coloured and glazed tiles

XXII. Part of a decoration of loops and palmettes from the balustrade of a staircase from Susa. Coloured and glazed tiles

XXIV. A pair of male sphinxes under a winged disc, from the Palace of Darius I at Susa (c. 490 B.C.). Coloured and glazed tiles: height 1 m. 22

XXIII. Part of decoration of a staircase from Susa. Coloured and glazed tiles

PLATES

1

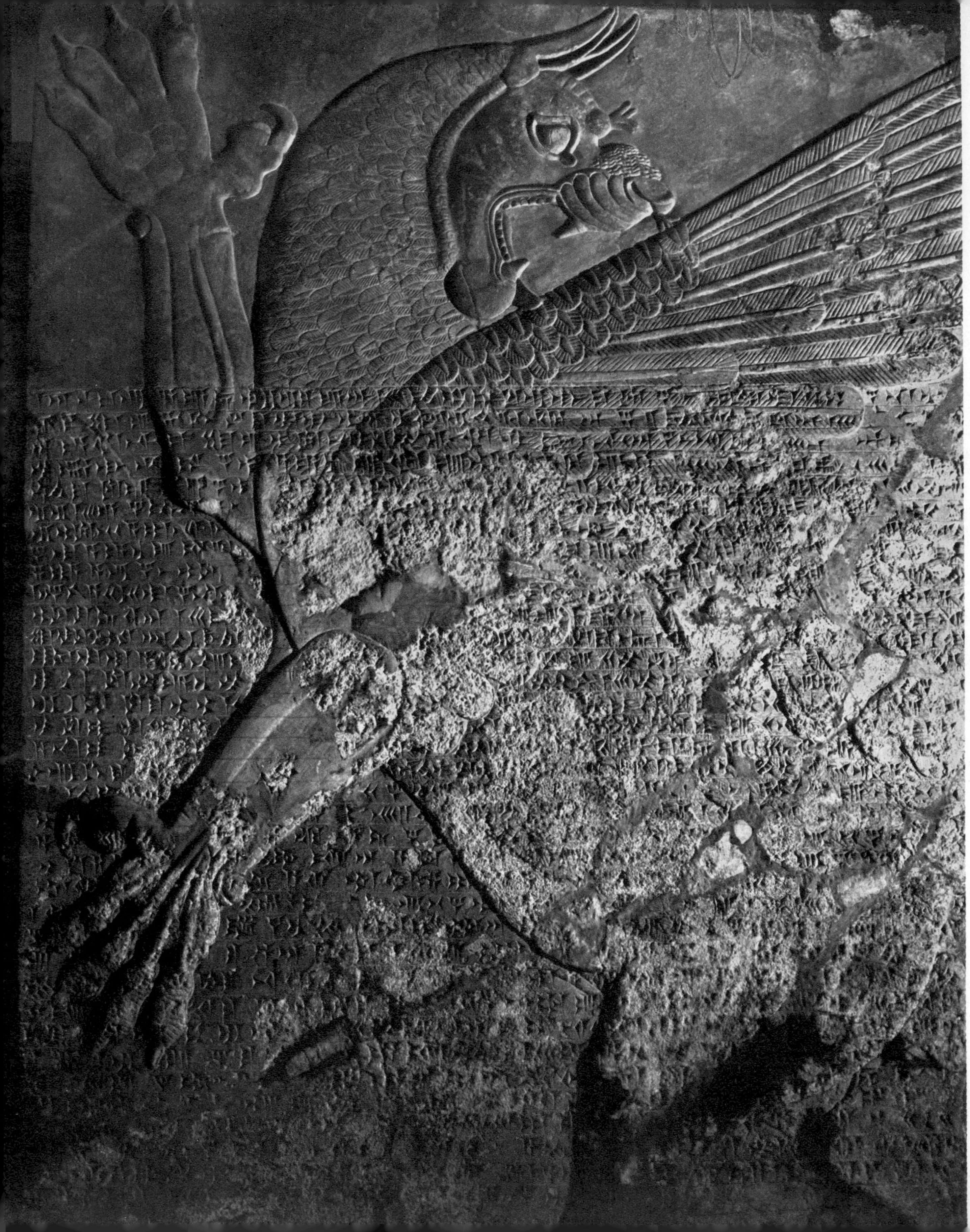

4

5

9

9

11

13

15

17

23

27

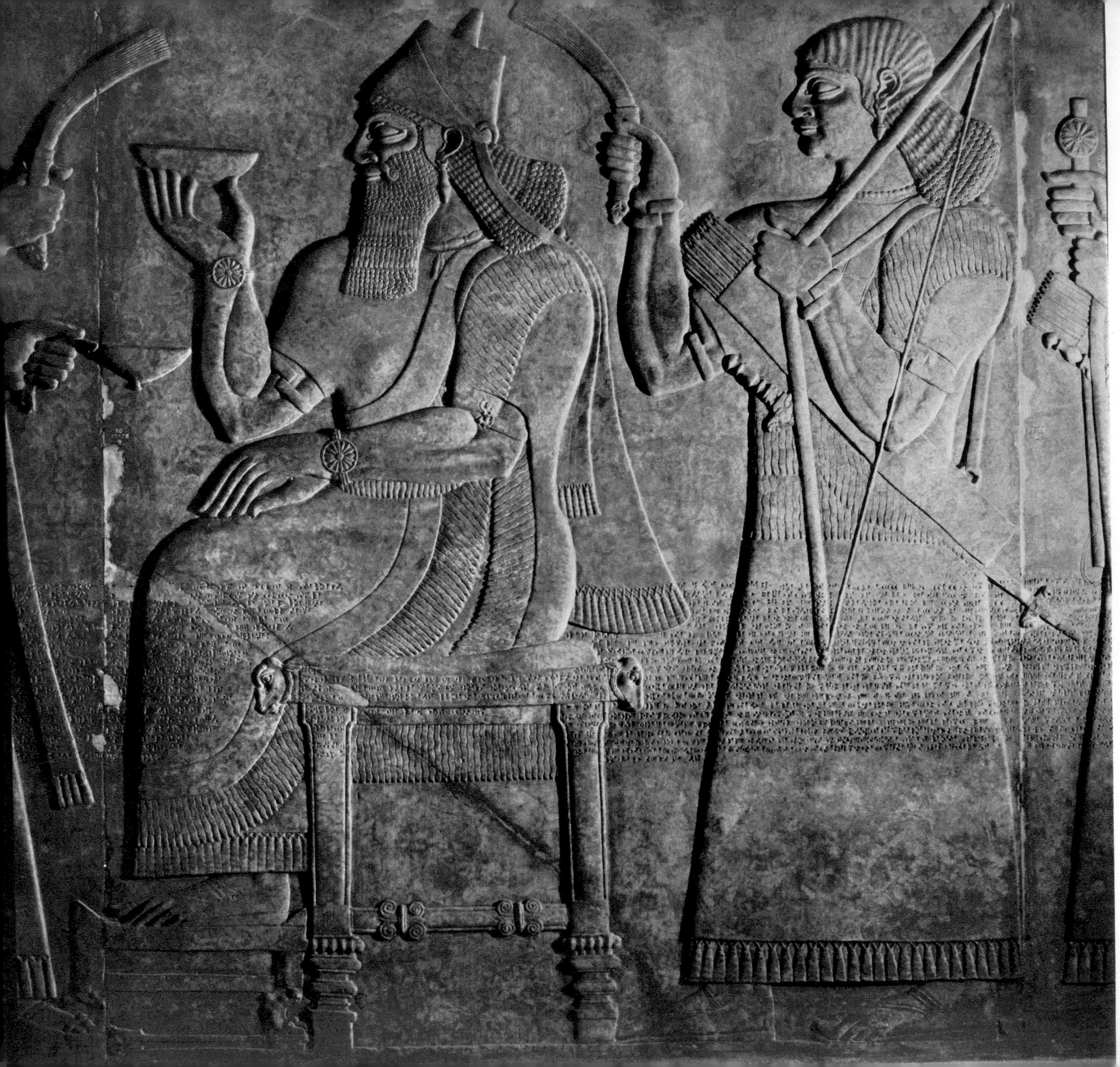

28

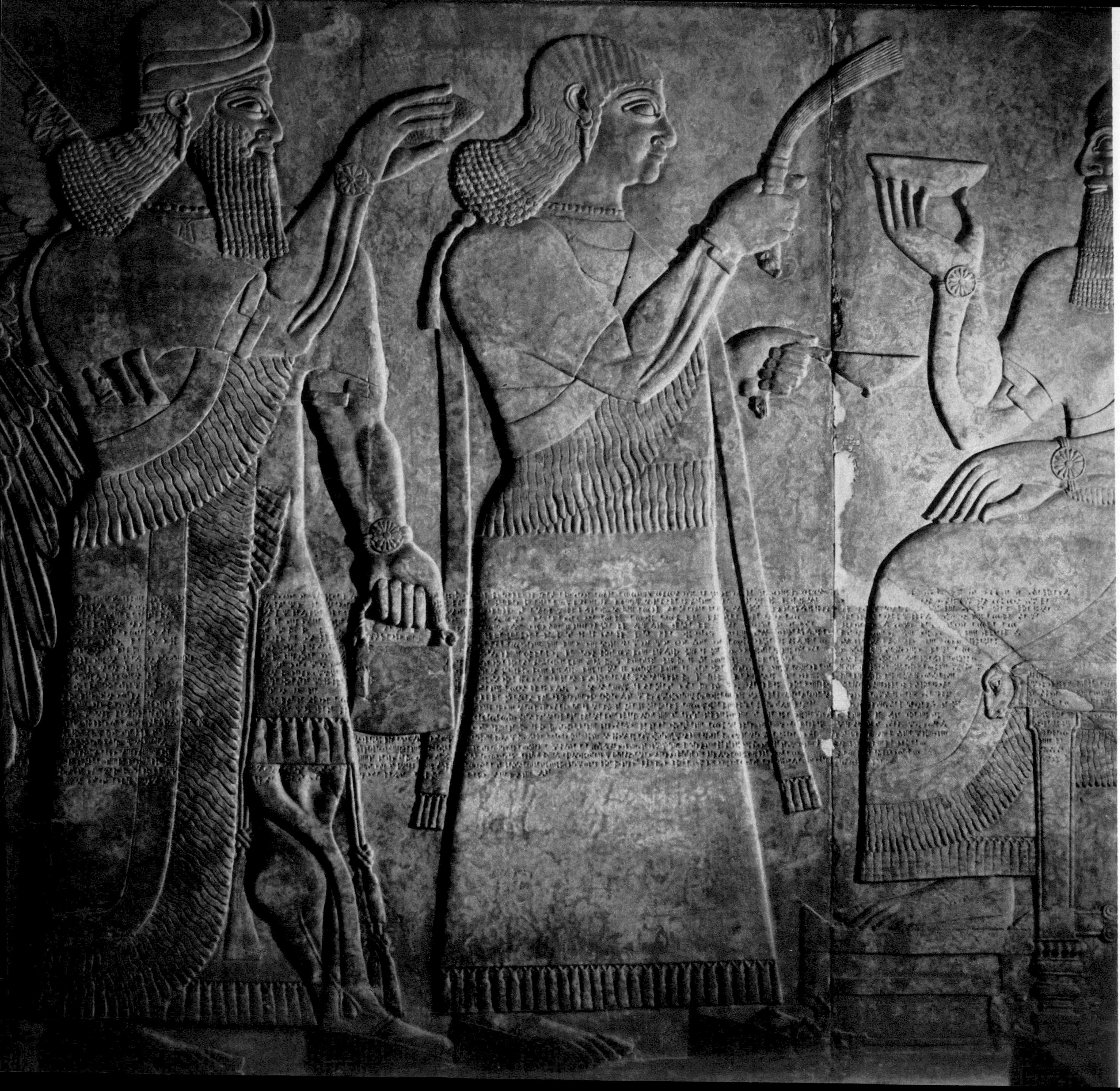

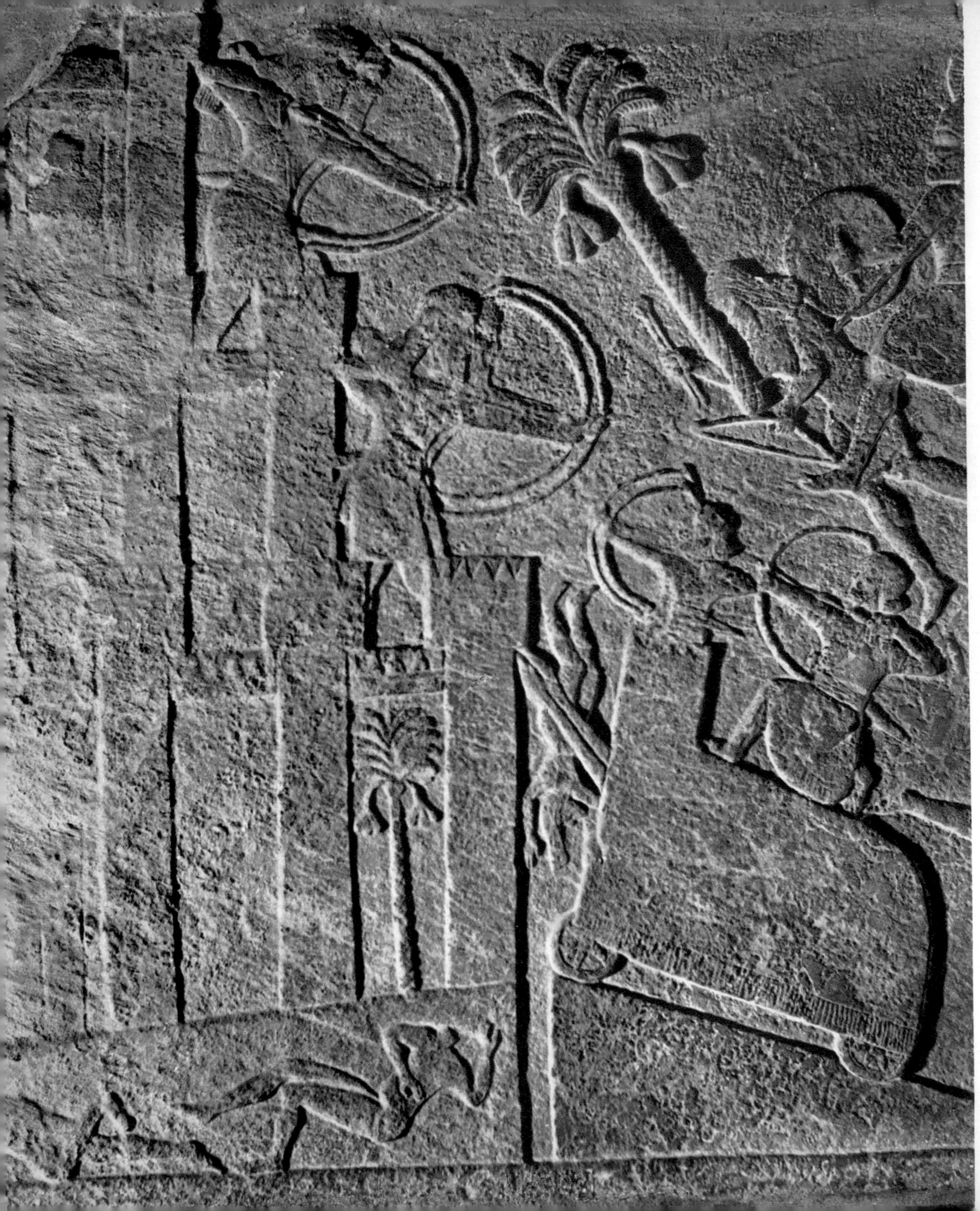

38

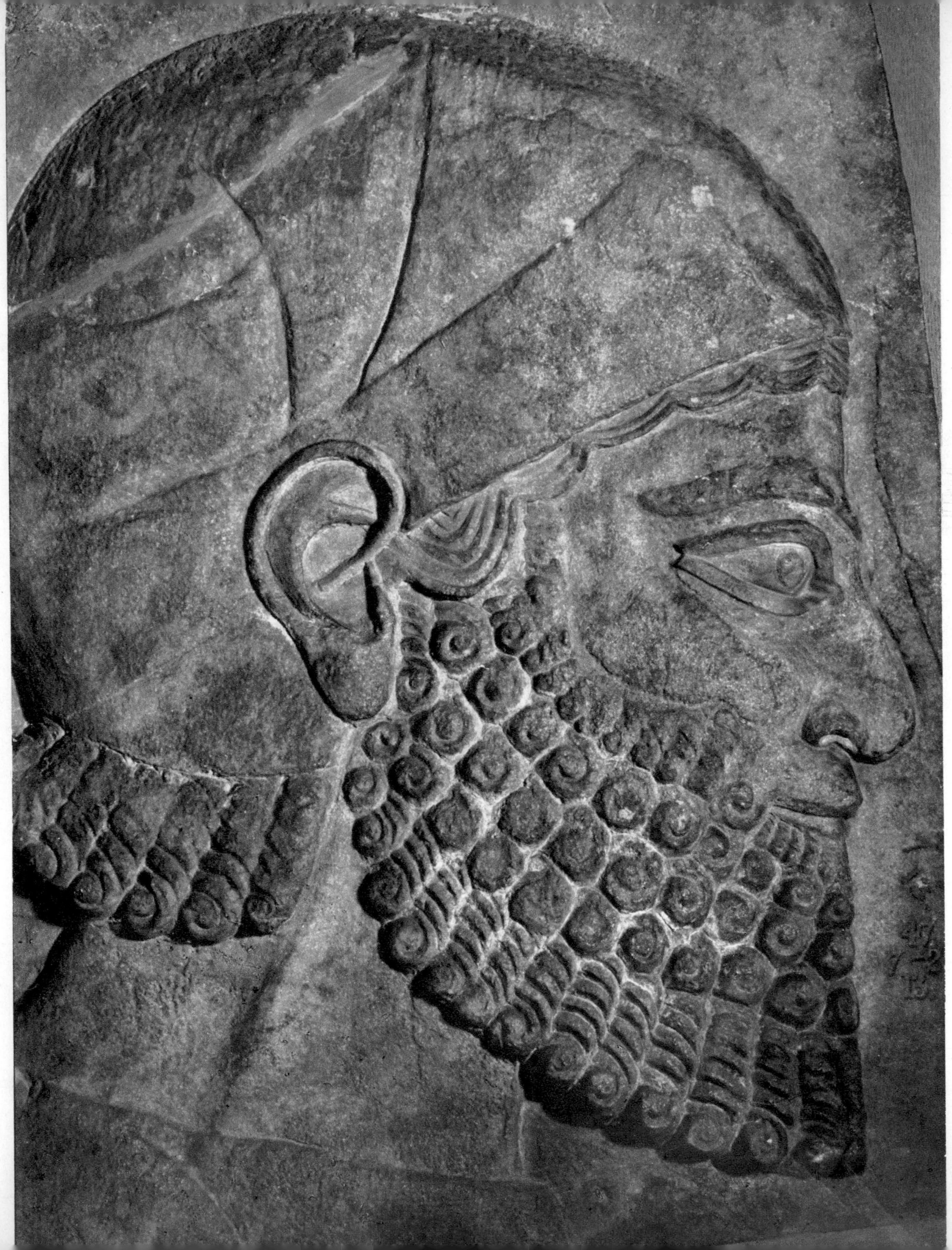

42

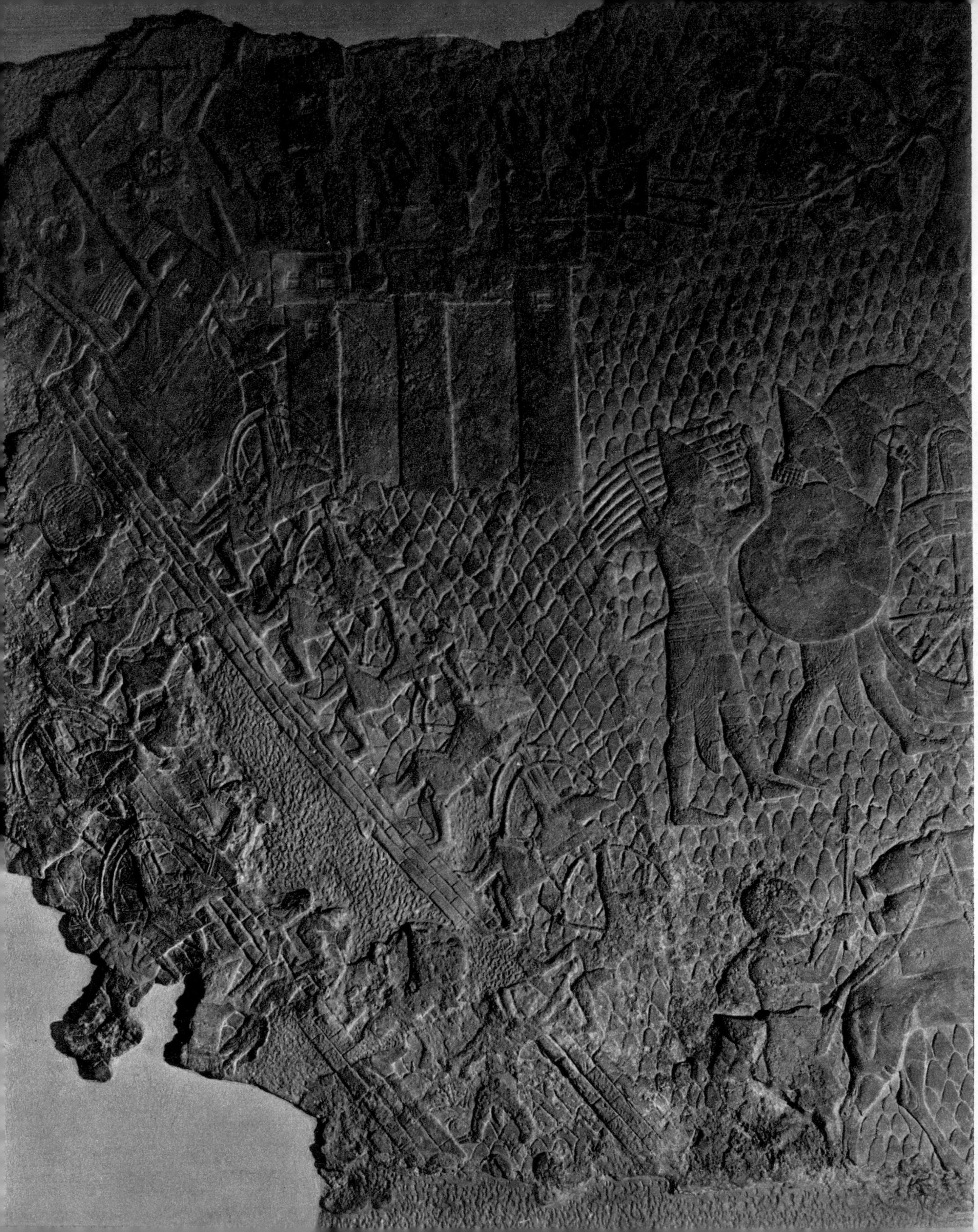

49

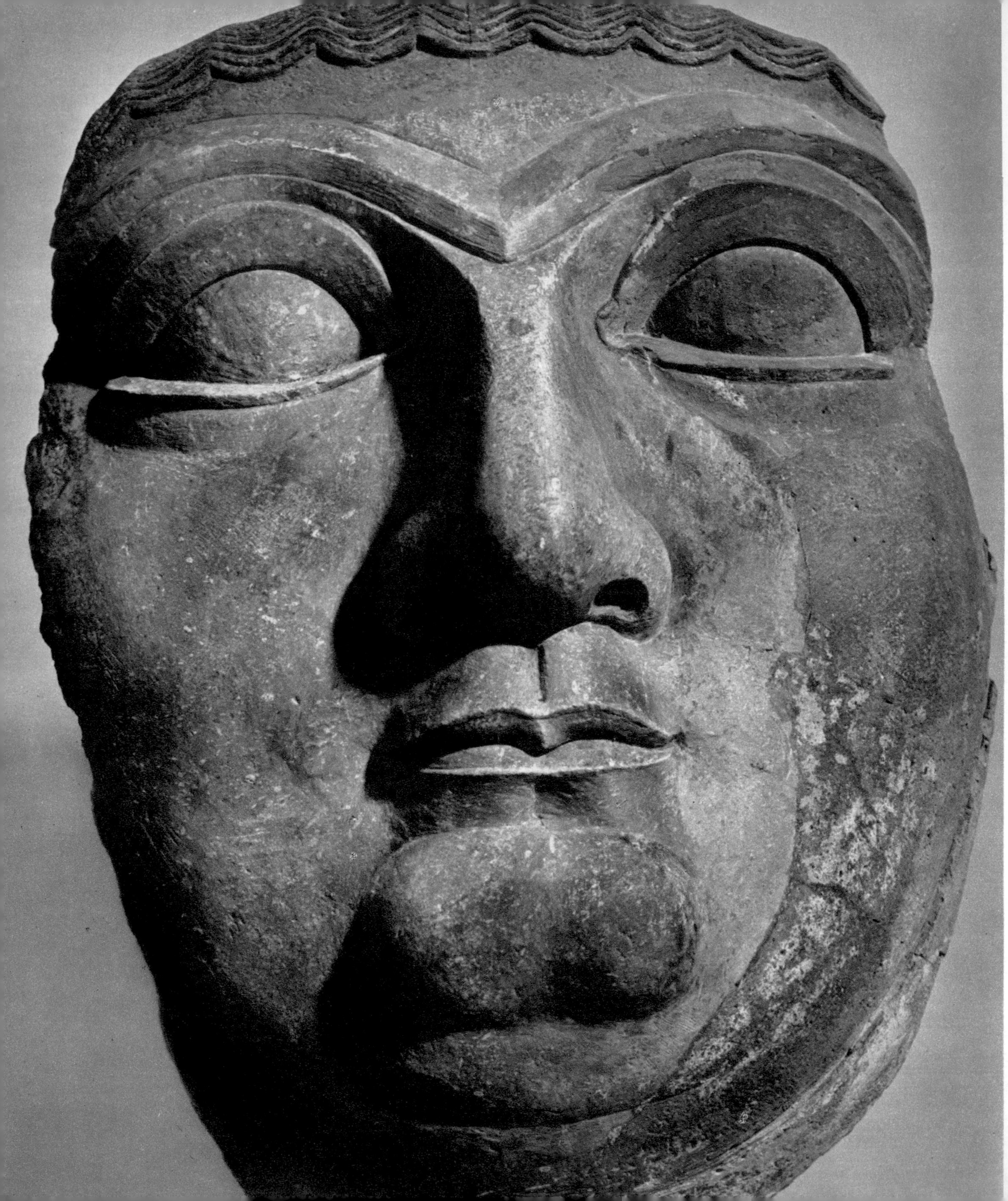

52

X

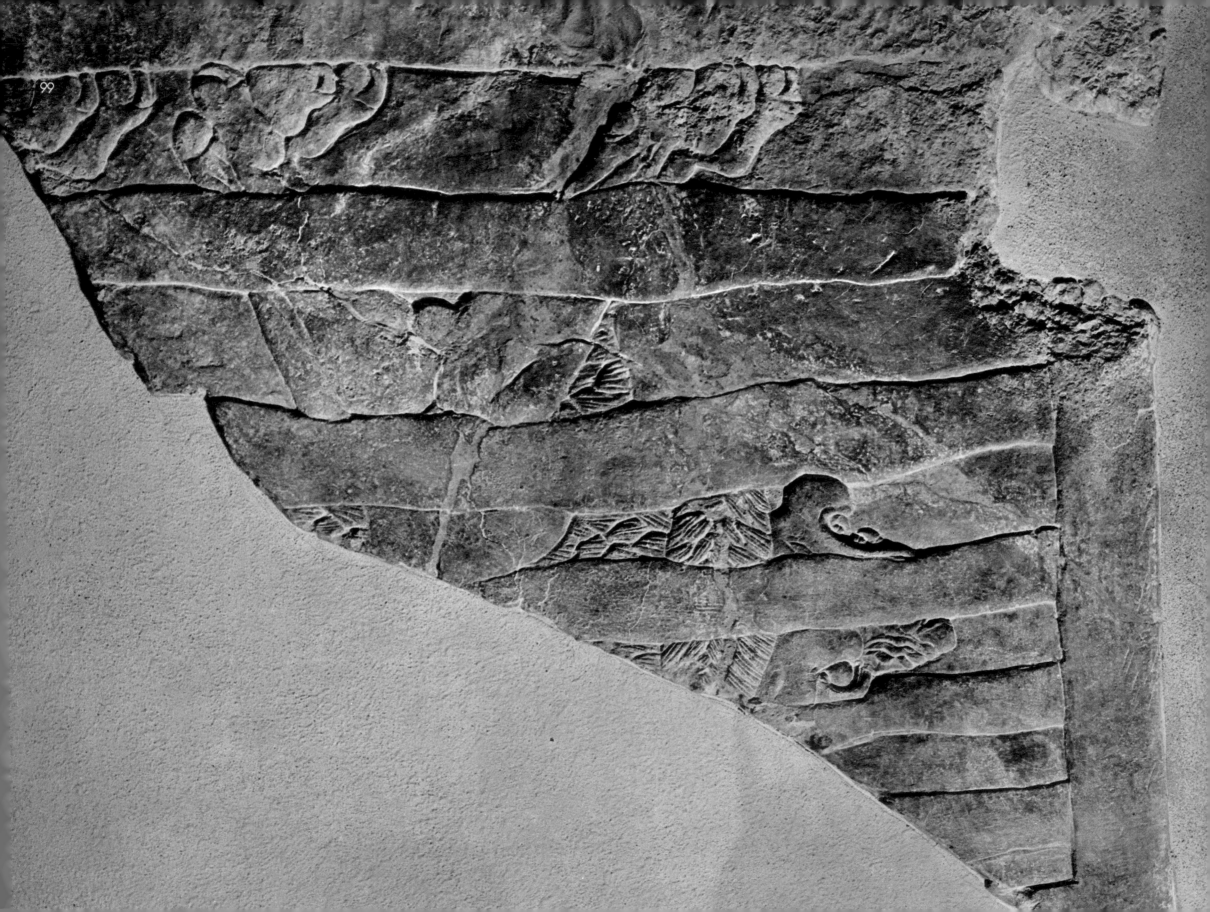

69

73

83

85

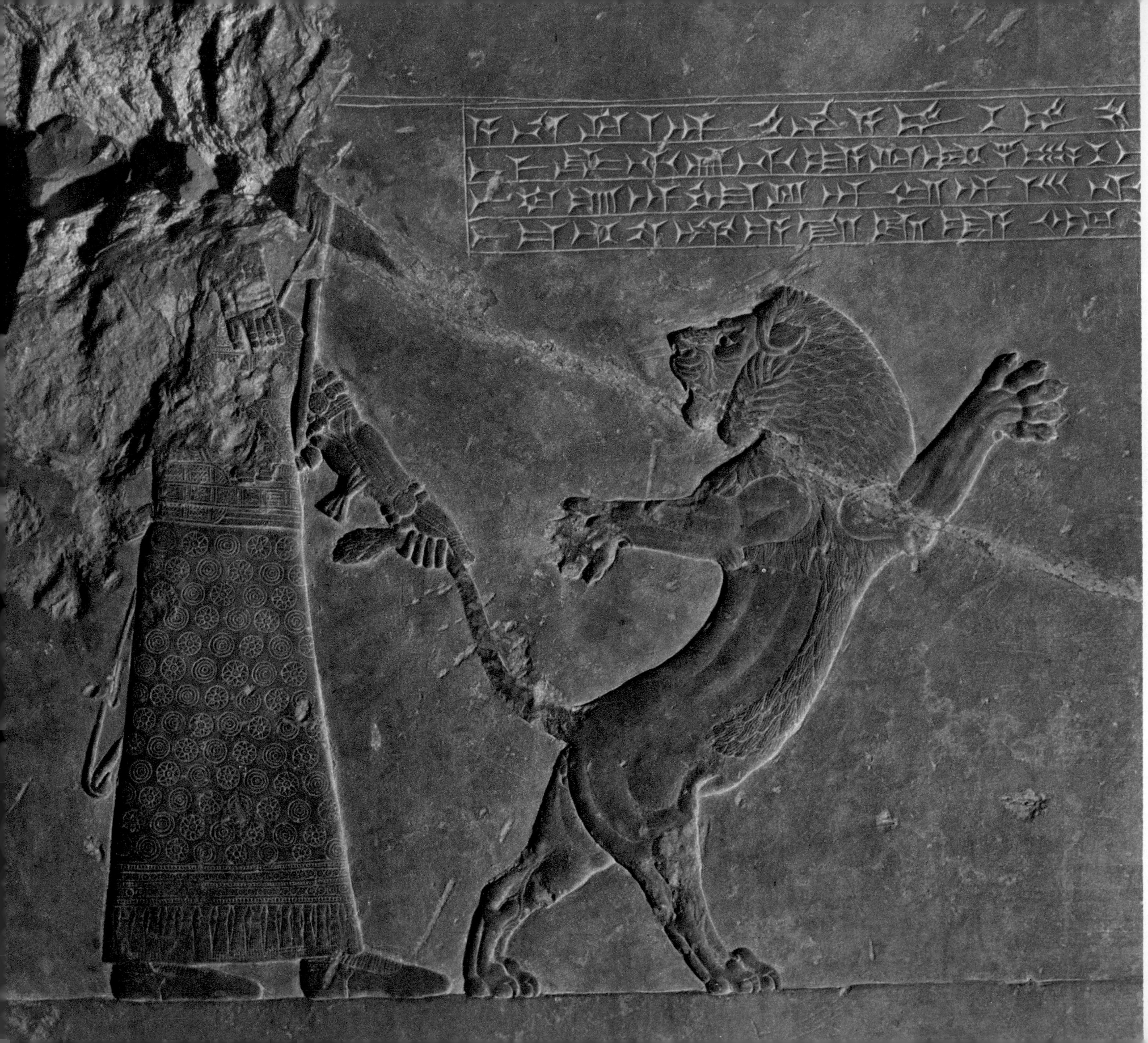

94

99

103

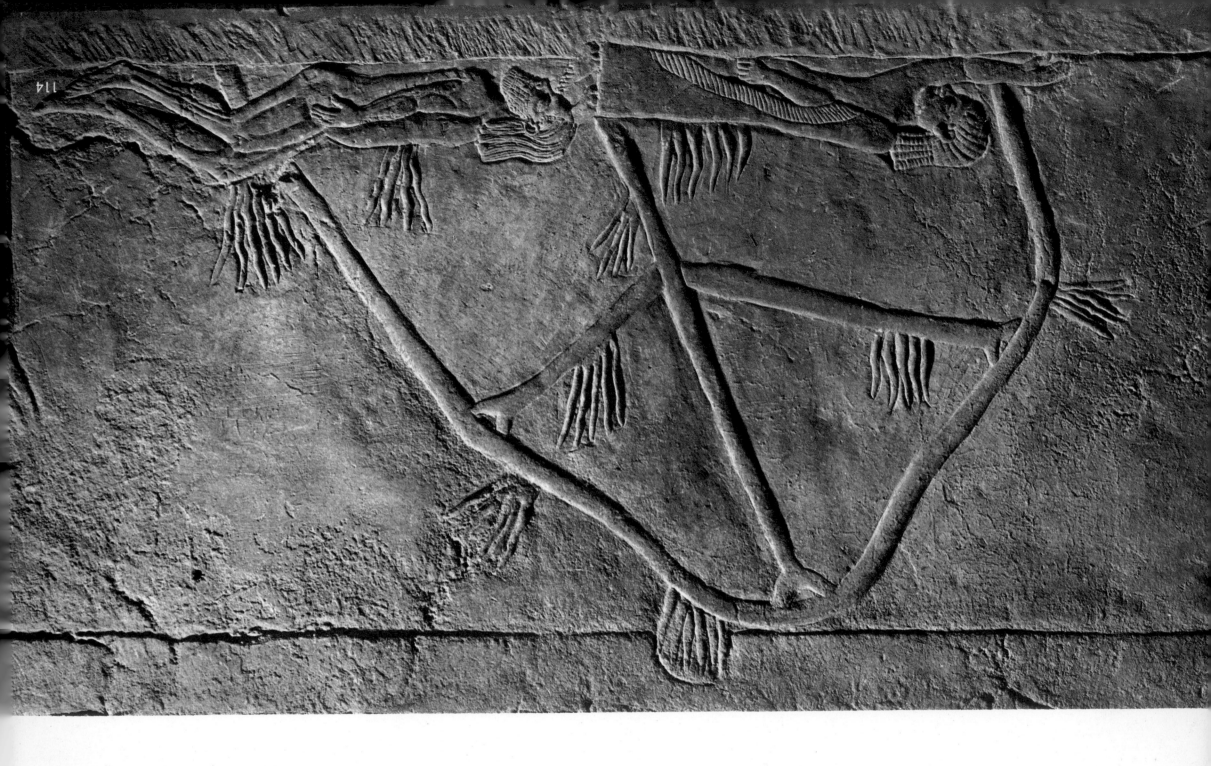

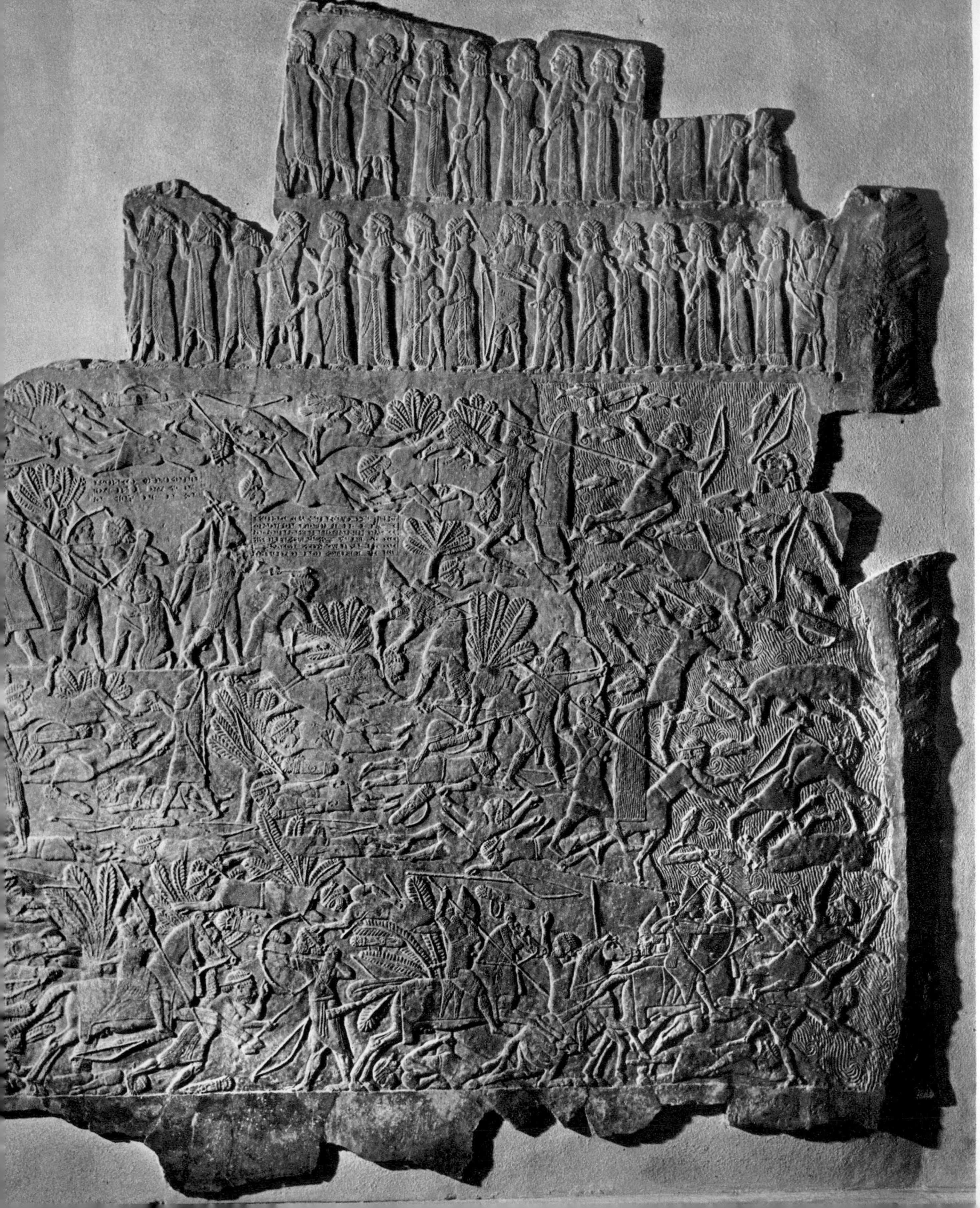

123

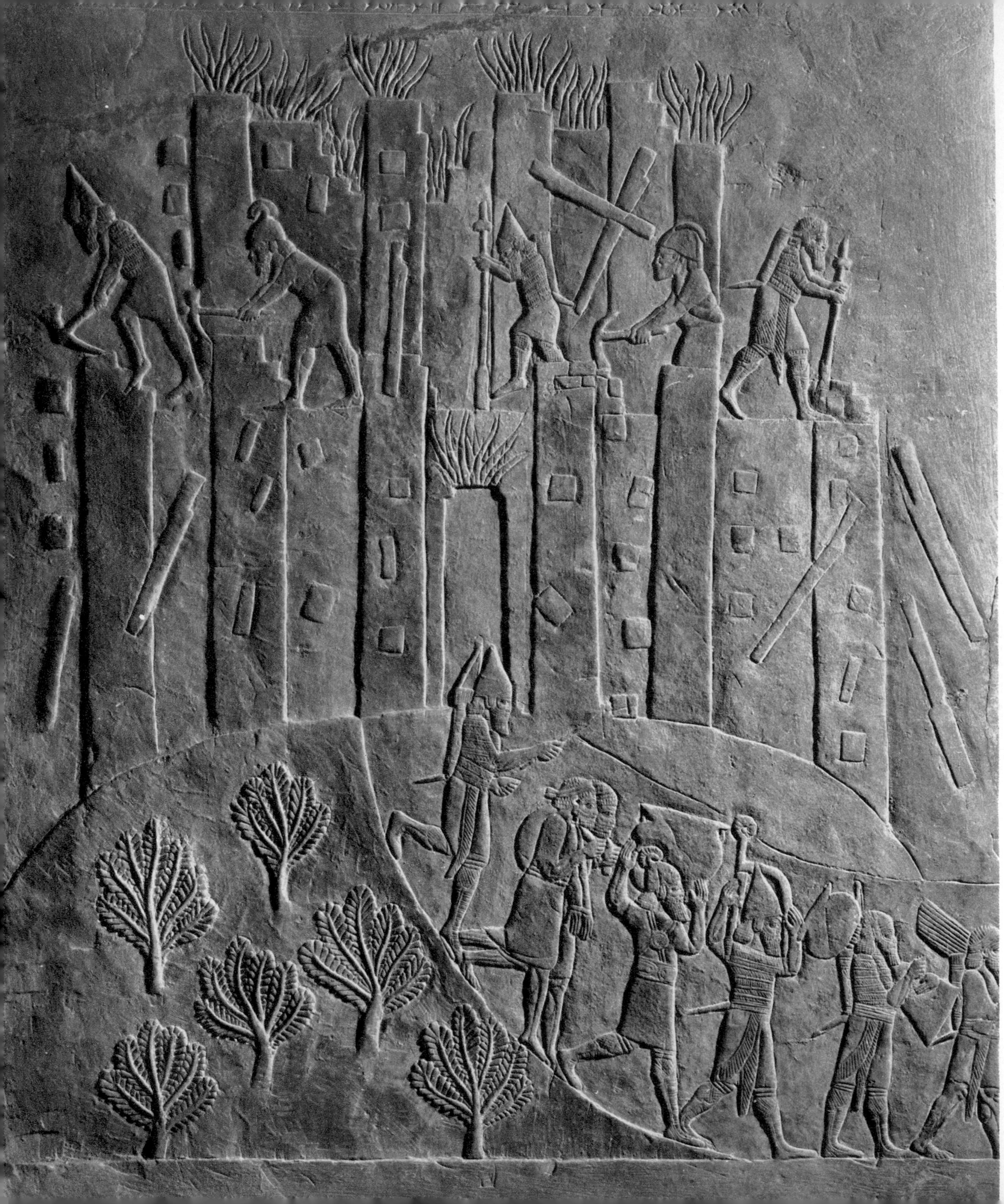

132

xx

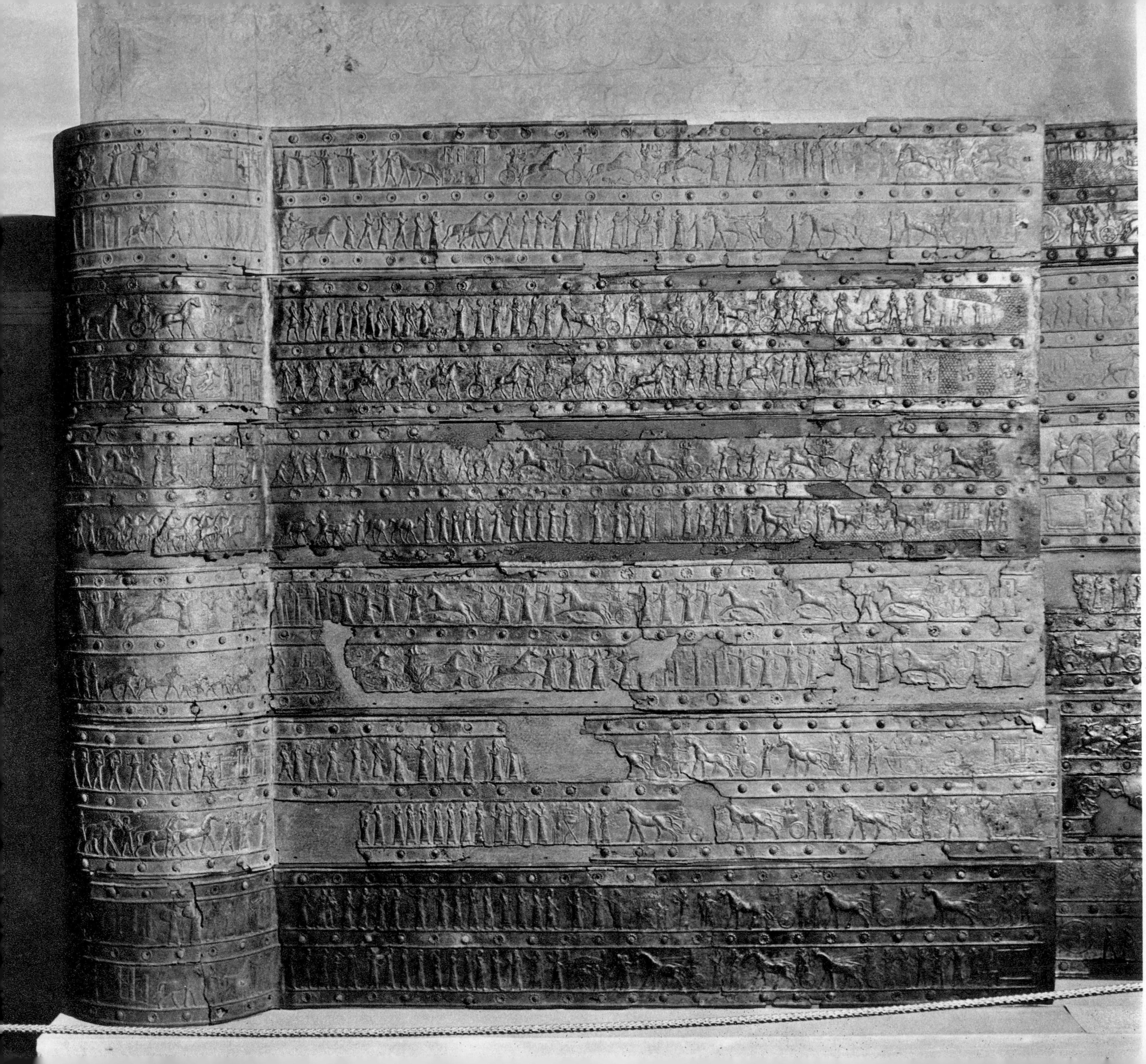

138

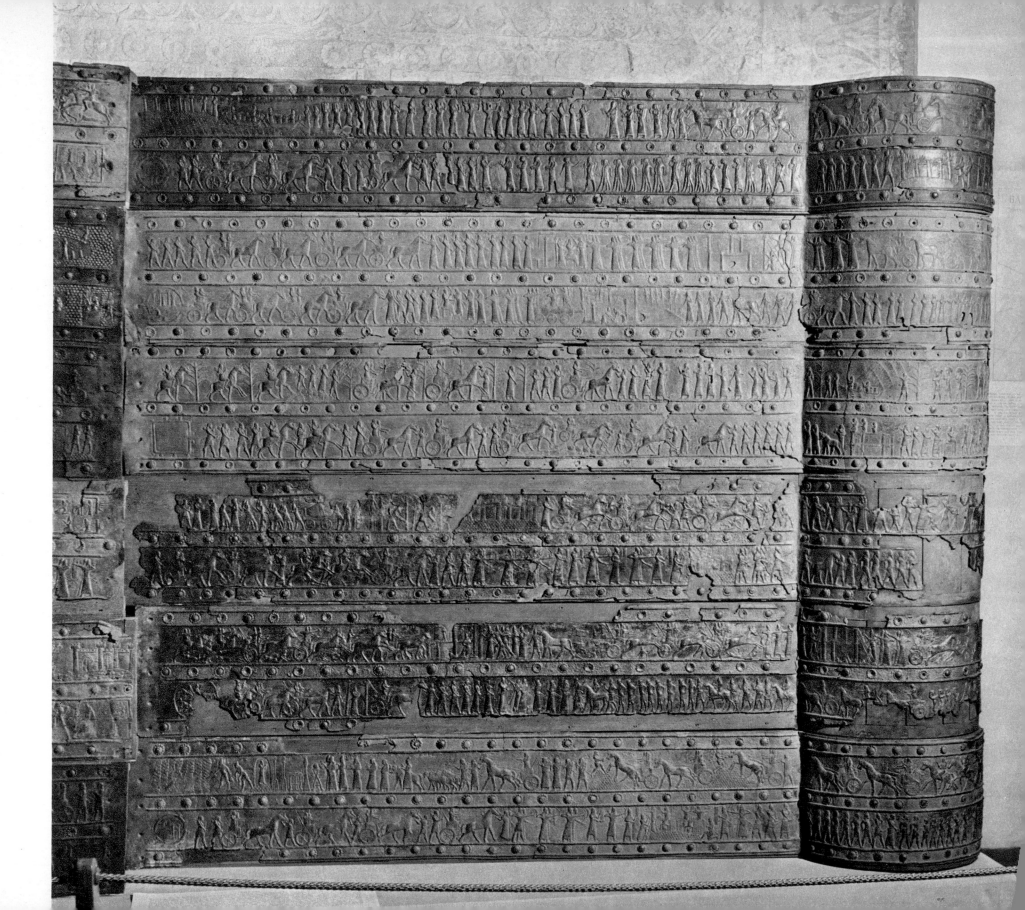

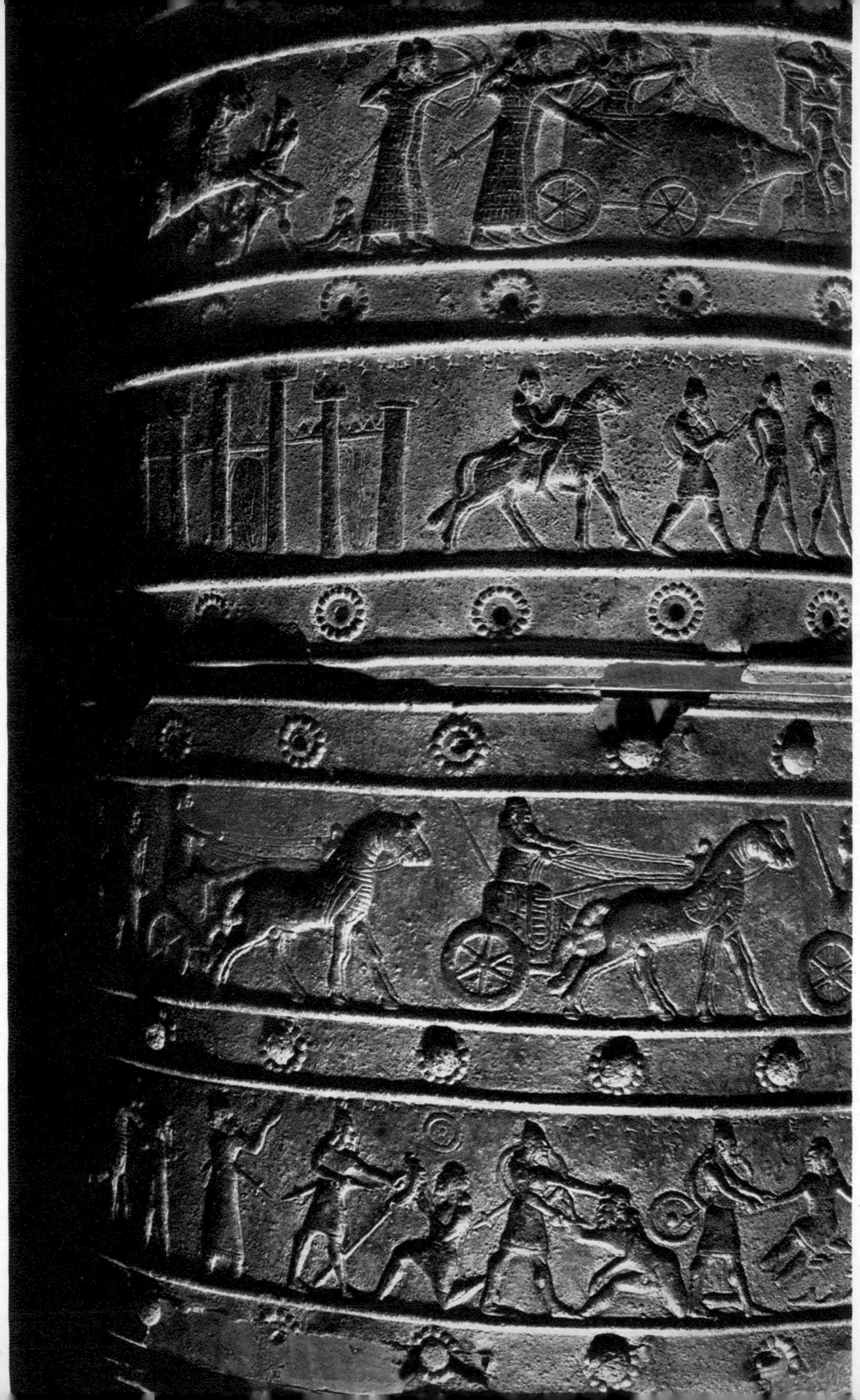

145

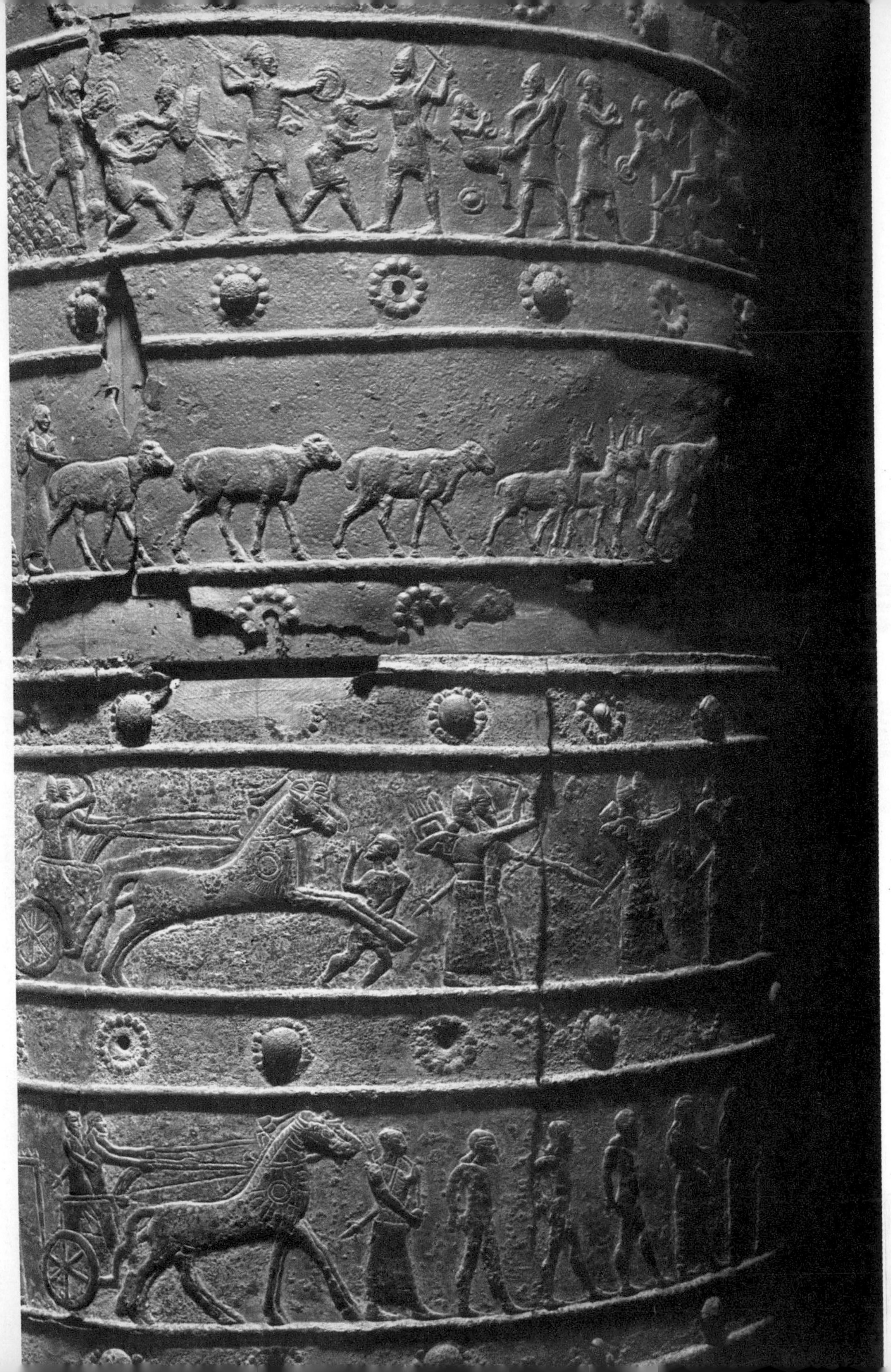

147

151

155

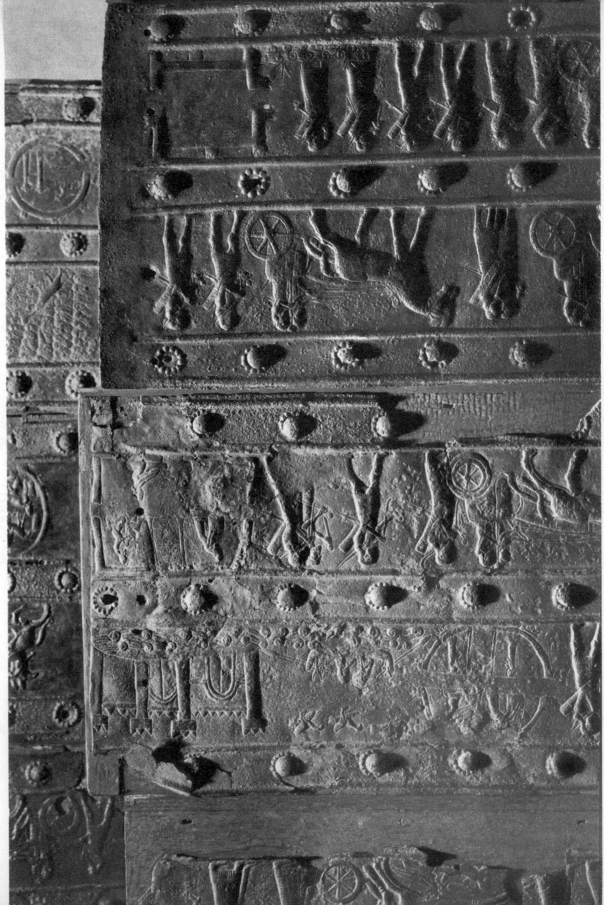

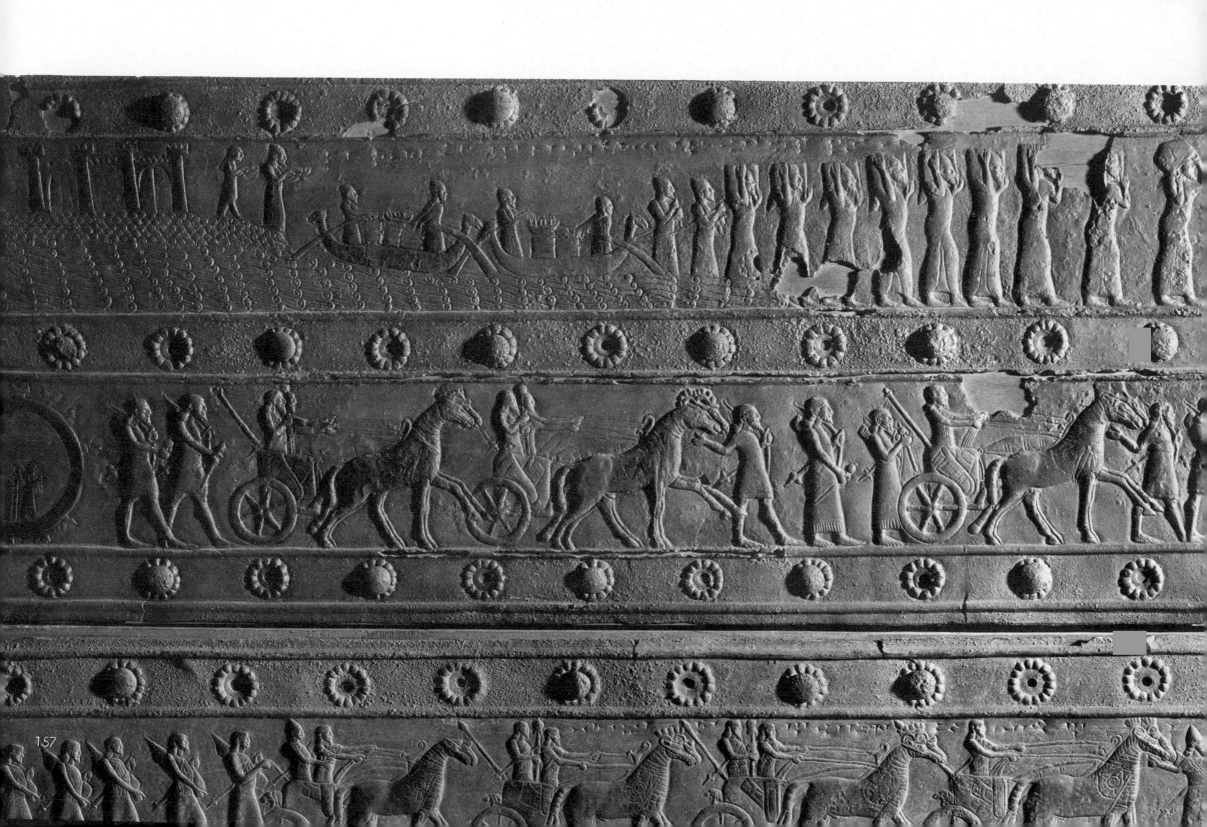

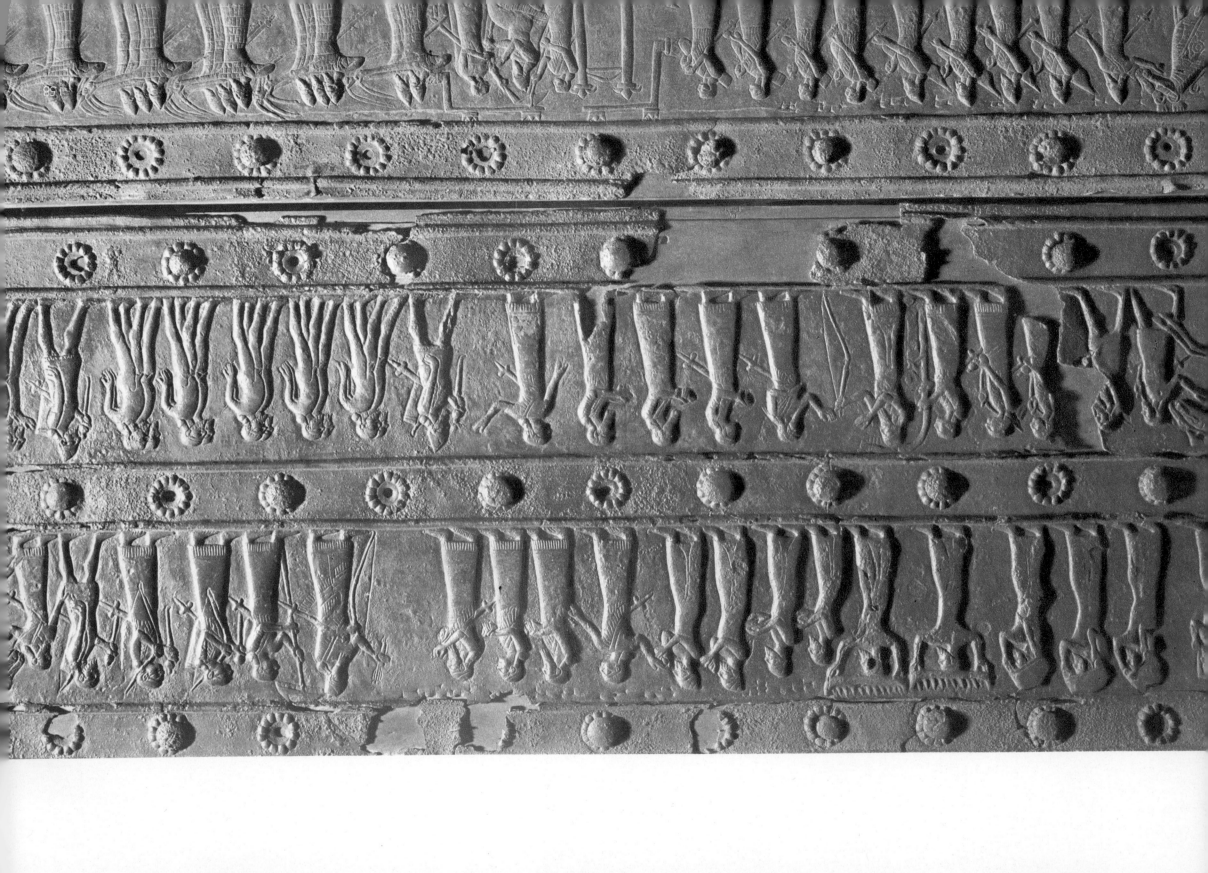

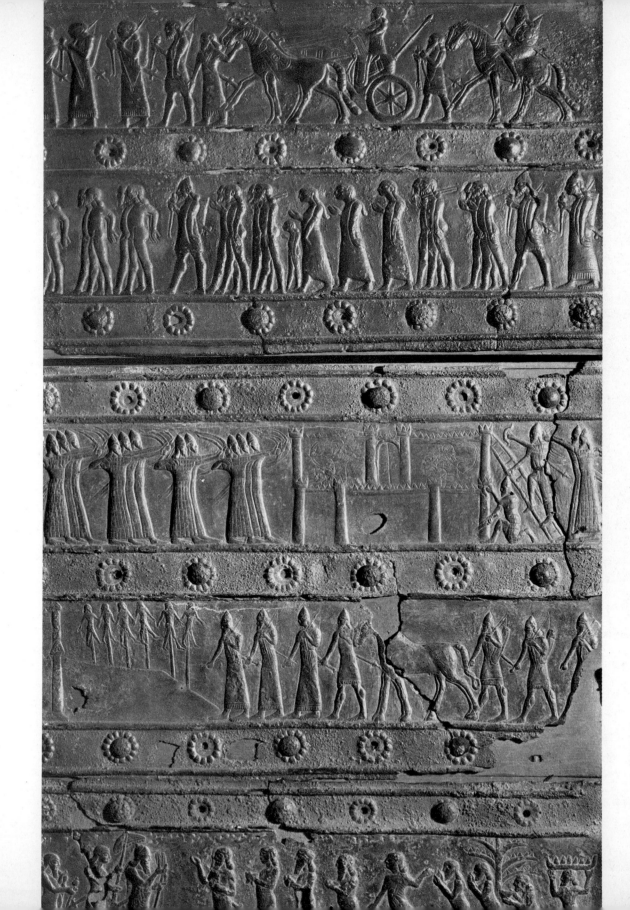

159

163

167